# EDUCATING HORSES
# From Birth
# to Riding

# EDUCATING HORSES From Birth to Riding

## PETER A. JONES

**HOWELL BOOK HOUSE INC.**
230 Park Avenue, New York, N.Y. 10169

**Distributed in the United States of America
and Canada by Howell Book House Inc.
230 Park Avenue, New York, N.Y. 10169**

First published by Rigby Publishers,
Adelaide, Australia 1978
Reprinted 1979, 1983, 1985
First published in the United States 1986
Copyright © Peter A. Jones

Library of Congress Cataloging-in-Publication Data

Jones, Peter A. (Peter Albert), 1936-
    Educating horses from birth to riding.

    1. Horses – Training. I. Title.
SF287.J64   1986   636.1'0888   85-21866
ISBN 0 87605 854 3

# Contents

# Acknowledgments

I would like very sincerely to thank the many friends and acquaintances who have contributed to and assisted me in writing this book. In particular the Directors, the Managing Director—Mr Colin Hayes—and staff of Lindsay Park Stud, Angaston, South Australia; Dr Richard Thornbury, B.V.Sc., for his expert comments and ever-ready advice; Dr John Kohnke, B.V.Sc., for his valued assistance with the sections on Feeding and First Aid, Rearing Orphan Foals, and for sketches G and I; farriers Gerald Ison, Roger Williams, and Les Marshall for their help and advice.

My thanks, too, for permission granted by the South Australian Department of Agriculture and Fisheries to use some of their material in the section on rearing orphan foals.

For the photographs which appear in this book I am very grateful to the following:
Mr Perc Kroschel, of the Barossa Valley Camera Club, for his painstaking efforts to record on film precisely what I required; he took colour photos 5, 6, 7, 8, 9, 10, 11, 12, 13, 18, 22, 23, 24, 25, 26, 27, 28; and photos 1, 2, 3, 4, 5, 8, 9, 10, 11, 12, 13, 14, 15, 16, 17, 18, 19, 20, 21, 22, 28, 29, 30, 31, 32, 33, 36, 40, 41, 43, 44, 45, 46, 47, 48, 49, 50, 51, 52, 53, 54, 55, 56, 57, 58, and 59.
Wm. G. Atkins Pty Ltd for the front cover and colour photos 14, 15, 16, and 29.
News Ltd , Adelaide, for photos 6, 7, 60, and 61.
Keith Stevens, of *Hoofs and Horns,* for colour photo 19.
Nona Jones for colour photos 30, 31, and 32.
My thanks also to other contributors of photographs and sketches.

To my wife, Nona, and children Mark, Derek, and Susan, for their encouragement and very practical assistance.

# Foreword

What manner of creature is this animal known as the horse! A creature that tests the skills of the world's finest artists, poets, and horsemen in order that they may portray, describe, or develop a relationship with this animal that combines within itself an inbuilt gregarious instinct with all the idiosyncrasies, fads, and traits of a singular individual.

Becoming a professional horseman—not from a philanthropist's viewpoint, or through the fantasies of wishful thinking or hearsay, but through the mill of experience and the teachings of horsemen who depend on the horse and their knowledge of him for their livelihood—has given me the opportunity or rather caused a necessity for me to study these traits and behaviour patterns.

This experience and study has encouraged me to develop a tremendous respect and admiration for the horse; his instincts pertaining to survival; his methods of learning; and his willingness to cooperate consistently when his education is advanced with an understanding of these instincts, and with consideration for his needs and peculiarities.

There seems to be no lack of books on the subjects of how to ride the horse and the advanced training of the horse, but comparatively little has been written on the subject of basic education in order to prepare the horse for more advanced tasks.

That is what this book is all about: to educate the young horse to a stage of being willing, safe, and a pleasure to ride. The methods described and portrayed in the following pages are derived from the handling and educating of many hundreds of horses including ponies for children, hacks for the showring, stock horses, horses for pleasure riding, and horses for racing—and here I must admit to a great interest, Thoroughbreds, for whatever purpose they may be required.

I trust you will find this book informative, interesting to read, and valuable as a source of reference, and you can be assured that it has been written by a person whose way of life is horses.

Peter A. Jones

# Introduction

The methods of educating horses to the requirements of man for whatever purpose man so desires—whether it be for financial gain, a passing whim, or a genuine interest in creating a liaison with one of nature's noblest animals—have been many and varied throughout the world since, according to historians, about 3000 B.C.

In this modern world, the age of rockets and the pioneering of outer space, the ways and means of improving man's compatibility with the horse during his basic education are still being sought.

In some areas of the world, where the horse has been held in such high esteem that he has been held on a par with, or even higher than, man himself, the treatment of the horse is of paramount importance. It is also a fact that in countries where horses have been readily available in large numbers, sometimes this consideration has been neglected. However, now that the demand for horses of most breeds and types exceeds the supply, it is evident that more knowledge is being sought to make the horse's treatment and environment a far better one for him to endure and to enjoy.

One thing is certain, the educated and tractable horse is far more likely to receive care and good treatment than the uneducated, untractable animal.

The main considerations that must be taken into account during the education lessons are the safety and resultant well-being of the horse, and the horseman, and that the education techniques have improved the horse's receptivity toward the requirements of man.

'Resultant well-being' refers to any particularly traumatic encounter between horse and man, resulting in injury and/or ill feeling, being indelibly ingrained on the minds of both horse and trainer.

Perhaps the biggest advancement concerning the safety and well-being of the horse centres on horses that are a commercial proposition, such as racehorses throughout the world, showjumping in countries where the prizemoney will encourage further competition, harness racing, etc. Money speaks all languages, and this is never more evident than when the person responsible for a horse has incurred the wrath of an owner, or his own conscience, when through an avoidable accident a highly priced animal, or an animal that has taken years to produce, is irreparably damaged, or even killed.

# POINTS OF THE HORSE

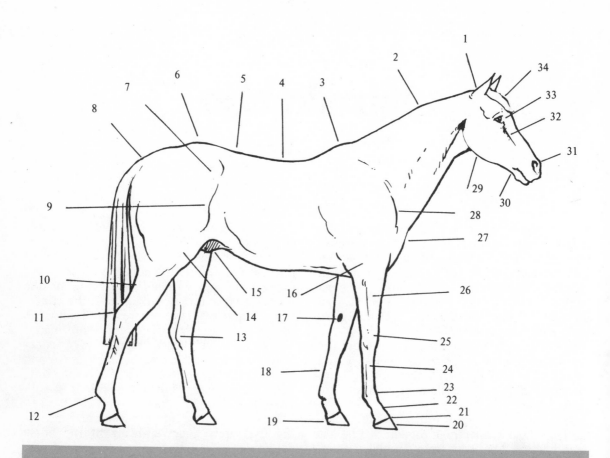

| | | |
|---|---|---|
| 1. Poll. | 14. Stifle joint. | 27. Point of shoulder. |
| 2. Crest. | 15. Sheath. | 28. Shoulder. |
| 3. Wither. | 16. Elbow. | 29. Jaw Bone. |
| 4. Back. | 17. Chestnut. | 30. Chin groove. |
| 5. Loins. | 18. Tendons. | 31. Muzzle. |
| 6. Croup. | 19. Heel. | 32. Facial crest. |
| 7. Point of the hip. | 20. Hoof. | 33. Eye. |
| 8. Dock. | 21. Coronet. | 34. Forelock. |
| 9. Flank. | 22. Pastern. | |
| 10. Gaskin. | 23. Fetlock joint. | |
| 11. Point of hock. | 24. Cannon. | |
| 12. Ergot. | 25. Knee. | |
| 13. Hock. | 26. Forearm. | |

# 1
# The Trainer

## THE TRAINER

The basic education of a young horse to reach a standard whereby he is at maximum receptivity to accept and respond to his further schooling requires the application of a combination of talents on the part of the person or persons in the role of trainer, including:

Patience, to the extreme.

Kindness, to encourage the youngster's confidence toward the strange and unfamiliar ways of humans.

Forethought, in that prevention is better than cure.

The use of psychology, in capitalising on a horse's natural instincts.

A sense of timing — which is the essence of horse education, in the application or non-application of any aid, manoeuvre, or sound.

The ability to convey, to create a rapport, no matter what the situation or circumstances or age of the horse.

Consistency is essential. A misunderstanding occurs if the horse becomes confused and bewildered as to what the trainer requires of him. This leads to lack of confidence by the horse in the trainer, with undesirable results.

Respect for the horse as a living being, with the right of an individual to question procedures to which he may be subjected.

One of the most desirable talents, and often the hardest to keep, is the control of the human temper. In scores of cases a trainer or handler is on the right course in educating a reluctant young horse to obey a command when patience reaches an end, tempers are lost, and the whole of the previous effort is cancelled out and often reversed in the horse's reaction. A traumatic experience brought to bear upon the young horse, by the direct result of a person losing his temper, is rarely erased from the horse's memory.

The trainer should also possess enough courage and experience to take the initiative, and/or take a calculated risk, should the occasion arise.

## INDIVIDUALITY OF THE HORSE

Although the horse as a herd creature forms regular habits and has a distinct tendency to follow or copy the activities of his fellows every horse is an individual — this must never be forgotten or overlooked by the trainer. There is no horse that is a set model or a certain vintage, that acts or reacts identically to circumstances or situations. A number of horses in a yard area are as infinitely different in temperament, mentality, action and reaction, and fear level, as a number of people in a room.

Research into breeding has shown a distinct

possibility that idiosyncrasies and traits, such as nervousness, timidity, and kicking, may in a large number of horses be hereditary to a degree. Much the same as the ability of some horses to gallop faster than others, or to jump better than others, is usually hereditary. Indeed, the whole principle of line breeding is on this genetic ability, the ability of the parents to transmit traits to their offspring.

An inquiry worth pursuing — is the horse that shows more resistance or reluctance in strange situations of greater intelligence than the horse who accepts these situations without question? The desirable behaviour is usually the latter, whereas familiarity and successful training of the former may result in a superior individual. However, the young horse is a living being and has a right to question the procedures and circumstances that he is subjected to by a dominating factor in his life, man.

## SOCIAL STRUCTURE

When two or more horses become associated an order of dominance and submissiveness is formed. This results in one horse being the leader or boss of the group, and the remainder exhibit a dominance of varying degrees towards one another, thereupon forming a social structure. This is evident when, during the young horse's education, two or more horses are required to work in close company. They will react in all manner of ways towards this association. It may be rebelled against in a violent manner, such as kicking or biting or, to the other extreme, welcomed to the extent that one horse will not proceed without the other.

The fear of the unknown will often override this social structure in a similar way that people with individual differences of opinion often combine or form a truce in order to face a common danger. The degree to which man can override this social dominance (for example, the application of a whip to a horse that kicks or bites at another horse while being ridden in company) is interesting. Also the question — to what extent does this level of individual domi-

nance or submissiveness in his own society influence his reaction to his association with man?

The trainer of young horses must realise that natural instincts, inherited traits, social structure, diet, and the behaviour patterns that have already been established by accident or design, present the trainer with a well-equipped and complex living creature, and the task of obtaining maximum control and receptivity poses a challenge of the highest order.

## SENSES

The four faculties by which a horse receives a trainer's wishes and demands are:
1. Sense of hearing.
2. Sense of sight.
3. Sense of touch.
4. Sense of smell.

The sense of taste also may be involved if the horse is offered food as some form of encouragement or reward. Although the giving of a titbit can be invaluable on some occasions it is not a sound principle upon which to base a horse's education. It is on the first three senses (hearing, sight, and touch) that control over the horse is based.

The sense of hearing conveys the voice and ancillary sounds. The sense of sight conveys the presence of people, location, and equipment. The sense of touch conveys the aids such as a rider's leg pressures, rein pressures to the mouth via the bit, etc. These senses are the three main mediums by which a trainer develops his control of the horse.

## PROGRESS AND PAUSE

The most effective reward or encouragement for obeying these controls or aids is to terminate the control or aid. Timing of the pause or termination or rest is most important. The pause, or termination of the lesson or part thereof, must coincide with when the horse is obeying the command given, to the extent where he is registering progress even to the slightest degree. The pause should not be made when the horse is in conflict with the command.

The most effective remedy when a horse is not obeying the controls or aids is the continual and quiet persistent use of that particular control or aid, whether it be a voice, rein, leg, or control of any description, until some slight semblance of obedience or co-operation is detected. These effects combine to form the nucleus of all successful horse handling. The horse must be influenced into believing that to do this thing will bring him peace; and the trainer must honour this belief and give the horse peace when he responds.

Photos 1 to 5 are obviously pictures of a farrier inducing a horse to raise his near foreleg; but they depict far more than that. They illustrate in classic form the procedure of progress and pause. This technique is used on any horse to establish the familiarisation of any new procedure.

In this series of illustrations the farrier starts the first step in the demonstration as in photo 1. He then progresses to the position shown in photo 2, pauses, then returns to the position in photo 1 and pauses, then recommences, and

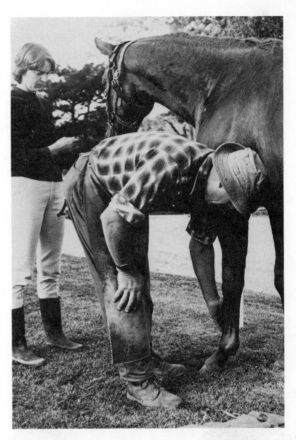

2.  The hand moves down the front of the leg, maintaining constant contact. A young horse will often accept contact down the front of the foreleg in preference to the back of the foreleg

1.  The farrier inducing a young horse to raise the near foreleg. In the first approach contact is made with the hand to the side of the horse's neck and moves down the shoulder

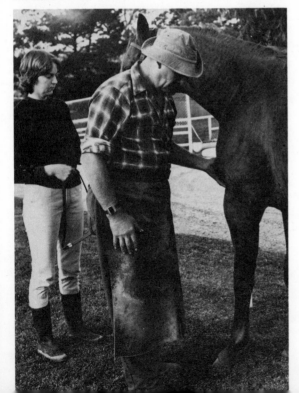

proceeds through photo 2 to the position in photo 3. He returns to position 1 and pauses, recommences, and again proceeds through photos 2 and 3 to the position in photo 4 — returns to figure 1 and pauses, and so on.

Once the horse has achieved a certain position well and the farrier is assured of the horse's acceptance up to this stage, for instance photo 2, in many cases he need only return to this position and pause. Should the horse take exception to any of the positions, or part thereof, progress is stopped, but quiet and steady persistence is continued until acceptance to that particular stage of the procedure is accomplished. Return to photo 1, pause, and recommence all over again. (See Appendix I.)

The key factor in obtaining satisfactory advancement is not to progress too quickly to the extent that the horse takes exception before the trainer terminates his progress for a pause. For maximum results when the horse is achieving that which is required of him, be it a minor response in the case of the first lesson or a major response in a latter lesson, the pause must be effected while he is doing the right thing, which then acts as the reward. However, it must be remembered that if the pause is caused as a direct result of the horse not doing the right thing, the reverse is encouraged. The horse will have received a pause as the reward

3. The hand has moved (maintaining contact) to the rear of the foreleg, with the thumb and forefinger applying a little pressure to the leg just above the fetlock joint. The farrier's right hand is pointing to his left elbow, which is pressed into the back of the knee. The horse is thus induced to raise his leg, it is not forcibly raised

4. The horse will gain more confidence if the leg is raised and lowered a few times before any work is commenced on the foot

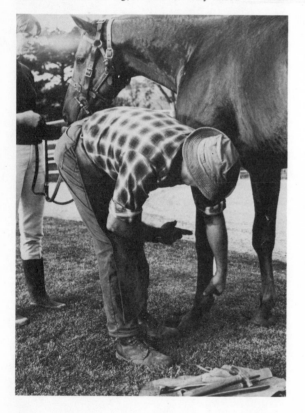

for his actions, but they will not be the actions the trainer requested, therefore the horse is being encouraged to do wrong.

The method portrayed by the farrier, the progress and pause method of familiarisation of any new procedures, is recommended for the education of the horse, be it approaching, catching, bridling, saddling, driving, or riding the horse, with two exceptions.

The first is, once the horse is familiar with a procedure there must be no excuse for him not to carry it out unless there is an additional element involved. The horse's reaction to an unfamiliar element being present in an otherwise familiar routine can change the whole aspect of the situation, as far as the horse is concerned. Repeating familiarisation with this new situation, using the progress and pause method, is then often necessary.

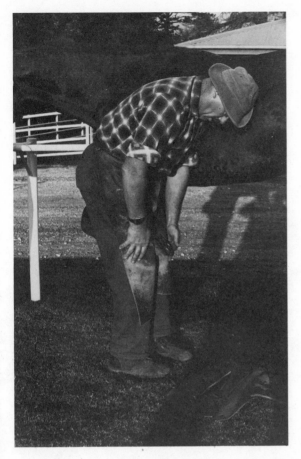

The second exception, and an important one, is due to economic necessity, which perhaps in theory should not exist in relation to a horse's education but in practice usually does. A number of things described in this book may seem to contradict, but they actually hasten the progress and pause method.

For instance, a transport may arrive to collect a horse, the horse is very difficult in allowing a headcollar or bridle to be fitted so, instead of keeping the transport waiting indefinitely, the progress and pause method is augmented by other and faster procedures for fitting a headcollar or bridle, etc. However, these augmentative methods are in no way detrimental to the progress of the horse's education. They are simply methods of hastening the progress and pause method to a practical level.

5. The foot is in position for the farrier to commence work. It is preferable to position the young, inexperienced horse adjacent to a wall or fence in order to prevent him from circling away from the farrier

15

# 2

# Handling Foals

## COMMENCEMENT OF FOAL EDUCATION

A horse that is well handled, but not petted, from the time he is a few days old, is far more receptive to man's wishes than the horse that is left unhandled.

If a foal has a headcollar introduced to him soon after birth (two days old is recommended), and he is taught to lead alongside his dam, it is the ideal age and method of teaching the horse his initial leading lessons (see colour photo 1).

The required forward movement of the leading procedure is accomplished by attaching a lead rein to the headcollar, and inducing the foal to yield to a pressure momentarily applied to him via the rein and headcollar. The dam walking forward will greatly assist in the foal's forward movement.

The foal's natural instincts of accompanying his mother can then be capitalised on. The timing of applying pressure, and release of pressure when the foal responds, is of paramount importance in effecting a satisfactory response. A verbal signal such as the words 'Walk', or 'Lead', or a clicking sound made by the

6. *Facing page:* Restraining a two-day-old thoroughbred foal by holding her with one arm around the rear and one arm under her neck. A lead rein being used as a Figure 8 restraint is in place but is not being used in the photo *(Photo courtesy News Ltd)*

tongue, etc., should accompany the use of the pressure. These signals eventually evolve as the verbal aids to proceed with forward movement.

The progress and pause technique is extremely important when teaching horses of any age to lead, or to improve their response to a lead rein. A pause must follow as the reward when progress is achieved, to demonstrate to the horse that to respond will bring peace. The degree of progress to be achieved before a pause is effected can range from the very slightest semblance of co-operation by the horse to quite a substantial part of a lesson, depending upon the trainer's ability to assess the horse's reaction to the trainer's action.

In climatic conditions where the mares and foals are housed or boxed at night, the daily procedure of leading the mares and foals to and from yards and paddocks (colour photo 3) presents an ideal situation whereby the mare and foal can be led together—as in colour photo 1.

This daily routine is excellent for the young foal to assimilate the ways of man. However, handling should be kept to a practical level as overindulgence in ministering can lead to a spoilt and sometimes aggressive youngster. Care must also be taken that the the mare does not take exception to overtures from man towards her offspring and bring her protective instincts into play by attacking the handler.

17

If the offspring should be a first foal the dam is quite often very proud and protective. A line of least resistance is best taken, with flexibility in the handler's action to educate the mare as well as the foal to the dual leading procedure.

This early handling does make it somewhat easier for treatment of the deformities, abrasions, and minor ailments that often occur in young foals. Remember that age proportionately increases the injury incidence, until the horse reaches maturity.

Do not forget the all-important process of deworming. One of man's greatest contributions towards the health and well-being of a horse is his ability to control the parasites, etc., to which a horse can become host.

Regular handling should, however, be continued for at least four weeks to have a lasting effect. In experiments in teaching foals to lead from two days old and leading them daily, a number of foals were led for one week and the leading discontinued, a number for two weeks and then discontinued, and so on, up to the sixth week. It was found, as a rule, that when the leading lessons were discontinued at any stage under three weeks, and not recommenced until weaning age (five to six months), little, if any, lasting effect on the foals' ability to lead readily had been achieved.

A leading lesson two or three days per week, for the first seven weeks at least, after birth proved very satisfactory.

Climatic conditions and the economic feasibility of labour often have a deciding influence on breeding establishments as to whether the horse's education should start from foaling or whether a more intensive education should be started later in life.

However, if the procedure of teaching the foal to respond to the rudiments of a headcollar and lead have not been carried out at this early age, and the foal is virtually untouched and a little too big to hold by putting one arm around his chest and one around his rear — for instance, a thoroughbred at approximately two months — he can be caught by putting the mare and foal in a confined space, similar to the size of a double space on a horse transport. Then approach the foal in a progress and pause method, talking all the while, until enough confidence is generated to allow the application of a headcollar.

## COMMENCEMENT OF A FOAL'S EDUCATION AT AN ADVANCED AGE

Should the foal's education be commenced at an age midway between birth and wean-

7. Restraining the young foal with a Figure 8. A lead rein is passed under the youngster's neck, over the back, around the gaskins, and forms a junction at the wither where it is held by the right hand. The handler's left hand under the neck will promote guidance and reassurance to the foal *(Photo courtesy News Ltd)*

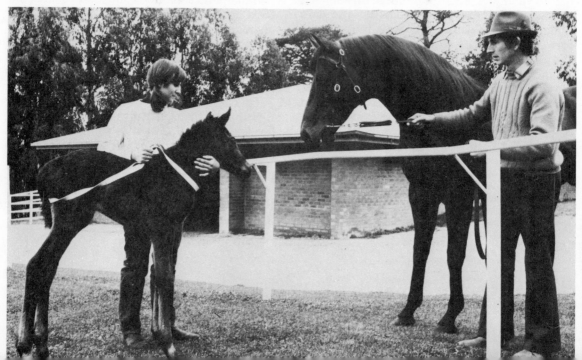

ing—for instance, three to four months old—the initial contact can be carried out in an enclosure similar in size to that of a double horse float. A triangular or oblong enclosure is best as this allows the foal to be confined, but not separated from his mother; indeed, he should be in contact with his mother when the initial advances are made.

The ideal equipment for the initial handling or securing of an uneducated foal is the double pen as in colour photo 5. This quickly places the foal in a very accessible and manageable position with the minimum of fuss and the minimum of risk (see colour photo 6).

Daily handling of the foal, commencing with the use of this equipment (colour photo 7), will bring him up to date with the early educational standard previously described.

If you want to catch the foal quickly, it can be done quite simply by having the mare and foal in an enclosure, as described, and then quickly grasping the ears of the foal, holding them firmly. As long as the foal is in contact with or adjacent to the mare, he will invariably stand reasonably still (see colour photo 4).

Should the foal be extremely big and strong and potentially capable of strong resistance an assistant standing alongside the foal, and grasping the tail close to the butt, will help the youngster to be held in a manageable position.

As long as the ears are grasped quickly and firmly, and the method is not abused, it will not cause any undue resentment if his ears are touched in the future.

This is also a quick and practical method of holding an unhandled foal while a headcollar is being fitted at weaning time. Headcollars for foals, or any young horses, should have plenty of adjustment. The noseband should have an adjusting buckle in addition to the usual buckle on the headstrap.

## VARIOUS METHODS OF FITTING HEADCOLLARS

The headcollar is usually fitted by inducing the horse to allow his nose to pass into the aperture formed by the noseband and chin strap.

Then the headstrap is passed over the poll behind the horse's ears, from the off side to the near side, adjusted, and then secured in the buckle provided. However, should the horse resent or not allow the placement of the headcollar over his nose or behind his ears there are other methods which will overcome these difficulties quite simply.

If the horse is difficult around the muzzle and nose area, the noseband is unfastened from the buckle and the headstrap secured first; then the noseband is passed slowly across the nose and secured in its buckle.

Should the horse prove to be difficult in the vicinity of the poll and ears, then the noseband is unfastened from the buckle and the headstrap passed around the horse's neck, approximately halfway between the poll and the wither, and secured in its buckle; the headstrap can then be slid up the horse's crest into the correct position behind the ears. The noseband is then passed across the horse's nose and buckled. When the headcollar is in position it can be adjusted to the correct size fitting.

With the fitting of all headcollars, bridles, etc., on young horses' heads, indeed on any horse, it is best to initially apply headpieces pre-adjusted to an obviously loose fit rather than irritate and provoke the horse by forcing tight straps on and over his head. One often finds out afterwards that the gear is too tight for a comfortable and workable position anyway.

Strap and buckle adjustments are easier to adjust to a correct or more exact fitting when a strap is being tightened rather than when it is being loosened.

*Talk* to a young horse that needs reassurance.
Do not be struck dumb once the horse has been caught.

Two farm owners were boasting about their properties. The owner of one property said: 'It takes me all day to ride from one side of my farm to the other.'

The other one replied: 'That's nothing, it takes me all day and all night to ride across my place.'

Whereupon a small property owner standing near by issued the *coup de grâce,* laconically saying: 'I had a horse like that once, so I sold him.'

# 3
# Weanlings

## WEANING

A major step in the life of a young horse is his weaning from his mother, usually at an approximate age of five to six months. This can be a very traumatic experience for the 'weanling', as he now becomes known. This time in his life can be made easier for him by, if it is possible, weaning two foals together.

The simplest method is to first make sure that the foal has a good headcollar, fitted correctly, then lead the mare and foal into a safe horse box. Lead the mare away and out of earshot immediately.

Two foals together in one box or small yard will find consolation in each other's company, thereby reducing fretting to a minimum.

Adequate containers should be provided for feed, although the foals usually feed satisfactorily from the one feed bin. The mixing of sexes at this stage is of little consequence. Occasionally one may bully the other and, if that happens, they should be separated. Wean in pairs, if it is at all possible, and the major objective of having the foal adjust to life without his mother will be achieved with a minimum of distress.

It is worth noting that the very first food intake that a foal normally prefers, after separation from his mother, is fresh or good baled green feed containing lucerne, clover, etc.

The box the weanlings are housed in has to be safe, with no loose buckets or feeders, and the doors should be floor to ceiling, or at least 2 m high. It is a pitiful sight to see a foal suspended over a low stable door, scrambling frantically to follow his mother as she disappears in the distance.

In some circumstances foals are allowed to mature alongside the mares, up to two years of age or more. But eventually the separation must come, and the older the young horse is the more mature his brain and the more weight he has to resist and fight against man's wishes.

The young weanlings seem to do best if they are left to adjust to their new experiences for at least two days, forming regular eating and sleeping habits. There should be someone just feeding and watering them (if they are automatically watered the vessels have to be cleaned), and adjusting their bedding (which should be copious), all the while talking to them in a steady and reassuring voice. All movements must be slow and discernible by the weanling. Be assured that the person attending to them will be under very close scrutiny, and memory patterns will be forming in the young weanling's mind as to whether that person is friend or foe, to be trusted or feared.

With the stipulation that the foals have already been thoroughly handled to lead, an alternative method of weaning a number of foals from their dams is to have a small number of mares and foals in a paddock and simply remove one mare a day. They must be taken completely out of the foal's hearing range, the most docile mare being left till last. This is quite a good method of weaning with a minimum of fuss and bother, the only problem being that the foals must be positively identified in some way, e.g. previously branded, obvious markings noted, etc.

Yet another method is to separate the mare and foal for a short period daily, gradually extending the time until complete separation is finally accomplished. A problem that can arise from this method is the continued stimulation of the mare's milk supply, but a decreasing demand. This can often lead to the mare having to be milked by hand after final weaning; quick and immediate weaning rarely causes this problem.

## CHARACTERISTICS BECOMING EVIDENT

At this stage of the young horse's development, conformation and characteristics are starting to become evident. The result of a certain male or female line may show in some foals being taller, or longer-bodied, than others of the same age, a similarity of heads, or white markings. And, most importantly, the temperament will begin to become evident, whether he or she is going to be nervous, highly-strung, impatient, forceful or intelligent, simple or inquisitive, or have a couldn't-care-less attitude. It seems one can compare them with young children; treat them accordingly and the easier and more responsive the young horse is.

When approaching an unhandled weanling in the box, and rubbing him down with the hand, reassure him that he will come to no harm. With two weanlings to a box, it is sometimes slightly more difficult to get the entire attention of the youngster, due to his association with his companion. However, the slight disadvantages of this are far outweighed by the advantages of having them 'do' well together for the weaning period, following separation from the dam.

This catching and reassuring is a relatively simple business if the weanling has been educated as a foal to lead. However, if the youngster is virtually uneducated, or has only just had his headcollar fitted prior to weaning, it is a more complex procedure.

## APPROACHING THE WEANLING

The mere presence of a person or handler within the vicinity of an uneducated horse confined by walls or fences must constitute progress. Therefore it must be followed by a pause, in other words, when a handler has entered the box or yard containing the horse he must pause, to allow the horse to accept the progress.

The horse's non-acceptance of this progress is registered by attempts at flight, and occasional attempts at defence (kicking, etc.).

The horse's acceptance of this progress is to cease kicking, or not to attempt to escape. To achieve this degree of progress the pause is effected, in order to allow the horse to realise that no harm has befallen him. The voice, used in a soothing sound, is of great assistance in calming his fears and is also the very beginning of a verbal aid.

The eventual securing of the horse is accomplished by a series of these progress and pause steps. The degree of progress is governed by the rate of acceptance by the horse. The degree of pause is governed by the time needed for acceptance.

The acceptance can be assisted, when approaching an uneducated horse in this manner, by a slight retreat in addition to the pause, in order to relieve the tension on the horse. If the progress and retreat technique is used, care must be taken that the retreat is not interpreted by the horse as his gaining of the initiative.

First bodily contact is ideally made in the centre of the side of the neck area, with the back of the hand. Once initial contact is made it should be maintained, firm and constant. Continue to maintain contact and begin to move the back of the hand in a circular motion in increasingly larger circles. Using the other hand, slowly reach to the elbow, then ease slowly up the wrist of the hand in contact until both hands are making contact. Still continue the circular motion on the side of the neck. The area of the circular motion can gradually be extended, until the hands attain a position to pass a rope or lead around the neck, or fit a headcollar.

The lead or headcollar can be fitted the first time this contact is made, or at any subsequent time, depending on the circumstances and the rate of progress.

## SECURING THE WEANLING

If the weanling consistently shows signs of panic, or kicking in a manner dangerous to himself or to the person involved, a quite easy and effective method of catching the horse quickly, and with a minimum of fuss, is to have the horse in a horse box or small yard; a horse box approximately 4 m x 4 m is ideal. Two handlers enter the box with a lungeing

rein, or a rope of similar length, having a small handhold loop formed at one end.

One handler takes the end of the rein with the loop, and proceeds to walk slowly up the right-hand side of the horse box or yard. The second handler takes the excess rein and proceeds slowly up the left-hand side of the box or yard. The rein, now being stretched across the box, is held at a level that is approximately 15 cm below the horse's muzzle (photo 8). As the handlers near the back of the box the horse will, in order to avoid their approach, proceed to the opposite side of the box (photo 9).

The stretched rein will be positioned to pass around the horse's neck (photo 10). Immediately this occurs the first handler gives his end of the rein to the second handler who quickly passes the excess and open end of the rein through the loop (photo 11) which, when pulled tight, completes the restraint around the horse's neck (photo 12).

Should the horse have a headcollar fitted already, the piece of equipment in sketch A will simplify matters considerably. It is a stick similar to a broom-handle, with a piece of plastic tubing or pipe approximately 13 cm long that slips snugly over one end. A piece of

8.  A rein, stretched across the box, is held just below the horse's muzzle

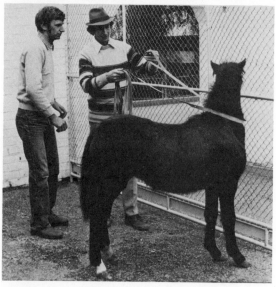

11. *Top:* The second handler passes the excess and open end of the rein through the loop

12. *Above:* The completed restraint

stout wire is bound to the outside of the tube, with one end of the wire forming a small hook and the other end attached to a long lead.

The piping with the wire hook and lead attached is wedged lightly on the end of the stick, the stick is extended at arm's length and hooked in the headcollar; the stick is then pulled out of the tubing, leaving the long lead attached to the headcollar.

When the youngster has been reassured, and contact is made with the hand, it is merely a matter of exchanging the catching lead for a conventional one.

Once a horse has been caught for the first

9. *Top:* The horse moves to the opposite side of the box to avoid the handlers

10. *Above:* The stretched rein passes around the horse's neck

time in a confined space, such as a small yard or horse box, it will be noted that the subsequent times he is caught, and until familiarisation with the procedure is attained, he will prefer to stand in the same spot as before, i.e. the association of ideas. If he is allowed to do so it will make the securing of the horse a lot easier. A short strap affixed to the headcollar ring under the jaw can assist in catching.

It is a good idea to repeat the catching of weanlings two or three times a day, and very soon the youngster will be nuzzling this person who has brought him little fear but has invoked his confidence and respect. The handling can gradually progress by familiarising the horse with the hand rubbing over the body and head, based on the progress and pause method, accompanied by talking in a reassuring tone.

When this is accepted and tolerated by the young horse the handler can then give the lead rein a slight tug sideways, so that the foal is required to step sideways in order to maintain his balance.

## LEADING

The step sideways can be used as the first step in leading. Immediately the foal moves in har-

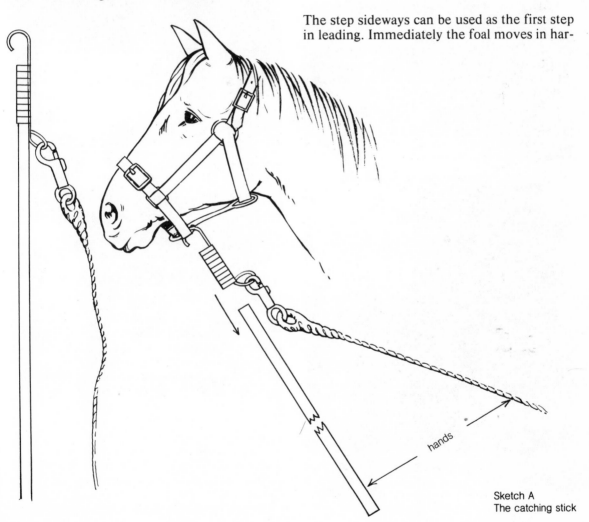

hands

Sketch A
The catching stick

25

mony with the pressure of the lead rein the pressure must be released. After a slight pause give another tug sideways on the lead rein, progress and pause, progress and pause, until over a series of lessons the foal will walk a number of steps in harmony with the lead rein.

The handler can now take a more forward position in relation to the horse, and an assistant can urge the youngster into forward movement. Alternatively, the use of the tail rope, colour photo 17, or harness, colour photo 9, can be used to promote forward movement.

When reasonable acceptance of this procedure is accomplished it is time for the weanling to leave the box and have a leading lesson or a tie-up lesson. Of course if the youngster was taught to lead as a young foal it is a simple process to lead him out of the box, preferably with an assistant walking behind him, and take him for a walk (see photo 15).

13. Encouraging a foal to lead light in hand. Pressure or restraint is removed from the lead rein when the horse is doing what is required of him

14. *Top:* Encouraging a horse to stand still light in hand. The weight of the hand is removed by lifting the hand when the horse is doing what is required of him

15. *Above:* A method of teaching forward movement to pony foals. The handler has his right arm over the back of the Welsh Mountain foal, his hand making contact with the rib-cage area. This contact will instil forward movement and encourage the foal to walk in a straight line

26

Care should be taken that in fear or high spirits the horse does not lose his balance and fall over, or be pulled over by the leader pulling on the lead when the weanling is not sufficiently balanced to maintain his footing. It is an extremely dangerous practice to try and pull the weanling forward by sheer force. He will invariably resist, and will counteract by running backwards until he loses balance and falls over or rears over backwards. Permanent injuries and fatalities resulting from this behaviour are much too common.

## TYING UP

It is a controversial point among horsemen the world over as to whether a horse should have a concentrated tie-up lesson, but it is generally conceded that a horse that cannot be tied up at the show, racecourse, or in transit, is at a distinct disadvantage.

A method of teaching a weanling, or any horse for that matter, to tie up, with the horse accepting the process with safety and the minimum of fuss, is as follows.

A chaff bag is brought into use, mainly because there are few items as strong and flexible for this purpose. Using approximate figures, the bag is folded lengthways, in folds 10 cm wide, until a strip is formed. The folds may be sewn together if preferred. Ten centimetres in from one end a piece of cord, 45 cm long, is tied securely.

The folded bag is then placed as in number 3

16. Forward movement can be induced by the addition of a long buggy whip or similar in the leader's left hand. The whip should be long enough to touch the horse in the gaskin and rear area (but not the flank). The use of this aid should be preceded, or accompanied, by a signal to move forward, enabling the whip to be dispensed with eventually.

Timing of pressure on and off the lead rein is extremely important. When the horse responds the pressure must lighten or cease, to induce the horse to lead light in hand. When a whip is used it is advisable to have the horse adjacent to a wall for the initial lesson to prevent him from swinging sideways away from the aid.

The photograph also shows a method of teaching the horse to accept being led from the bit ring when he has previously been led only from a headcollar or halter: the lead rein is passed through the bit ring, on the near side, and then attached to the headcollar

of sketch B. The cord is wrapped tightly around the two ends of the folded bag, leaving a space of about the thickness of a clenched hand between the secured bag and the weanling's throat. The tie-up rope is then introduced and folded around the bag as in the completed tie.

There are many variations of tie-up gear, some good, some hazardous. The above method is easy, reliable, and safe.

Should an occasion arise that the weanling must be given a tie-up lesson before he is familiar with the leading procedure, or that the

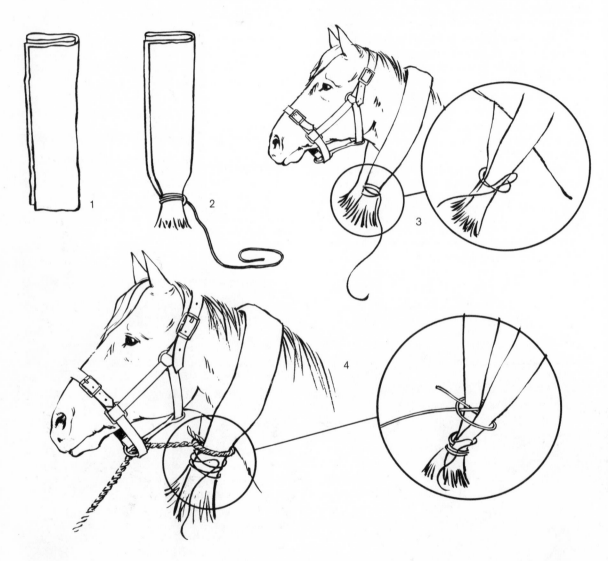

Sketch B
When tied in this manner the neck bag can be adjusted to fit any neck size. Its removal is simple and quick; the end of the cord is given a tug, thus releasing the two ends of the bag which, in turn, is simply pulled apart. The tie-up rope folded around the ends of the bag can then be removed

28

tie-up lesson be given as the preliminary to the leading procedure, the following method is recommended.

## TRANSFERRING A WEANLING

In most cases the weanling has to be taken to the sand ring or yard where he is to be handled, as these areas seldom adjoin the box. It is often hazardous transferring a weanling from the box if he has not previously been taught to lead. However, to minimise this hazard a 'coacher' is enlisted to assist.

A coacher is an old or quiet horse, or one that does not have a tendency to kick. The coacher is backed into the doorway of the box containing the weanling. The weaner is then allowed to sniff and nuzzle the flanks or hind-quarters of the coacher; thirty seconds is usually sufficient time to identify a fellow, but senior, creature. Identifying is sometimes accompanied by an opening and closing of the weanling's mouth in a peculiar snapping action: This is a physical sign of the young horse's conceding seniority and/or sub-missiveness toward an older or larger animal.

The coacher is led from the box to the yard with the trainer allowing the weanling to follow and holding the tie-up rope loosely as in colour photo 10.

Before proceeding further the apparatus to which the weanling is going to be tied will be described. Horses have been tied up to just about everything that protrudes out of the earth. However, the equipment shown in colour photo 12 is possibly the best so far devised for the horse and trainer; it is unique in that it provides comparative safety for a person standing in front of the horse.

The tie-up rope is wrapped twice around the rail that is exposed and not tied, but clipped in a clam fastening (sketch C) which is used extensively in yachting. The rope, in this instance 18 mm thick, can be released instantly by pulling it upwards.

When the coacher and weanling enter the sand ring the coacher is led to the tie-up rail and remains there while the youngster is secured to the rail. It is amazing how the close presence of one old, quiet horse will prevent a lot of fright, and panic, that young horses often display the first time they are tied up.

If it has not been done previously, the rear harness is fitted immediately the weanling is

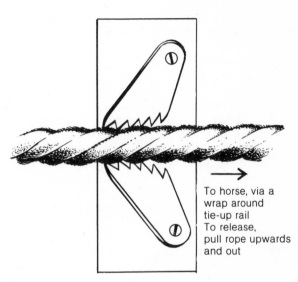

To horse, via a wrap around tie-up rail
To release, pull rope upwards and out

Sketch C
A clam fastener, which allows immediate release by lifting the rope up and out of the clams

secured to the rail. This harness is easily applied and removed and its purpose is to relieve the pressure on the horse's neck caused by his pulling. The adjustable rope is tightened so that the harness strap fits snugly when the horse is standing normally.

With the coacher still standing close by, the weanling is then rubbed all over by hand —slowly at first, until the horse accepts it without signs of fright and flinching. A saddle cloth or similar is then rubbed over him, until he is accustomed to things other than a person's hand.

When the weanling accepts this handling while tied, the coacher is then led away and the rubbing and the fondling repeated. Attention should be paid to rubbing the legs, right down to the hoof. The horse need not be made to hold his legs up at this stage; it is better to leave this procedure to a later date than to make an issue of it the first time the youngster is tied up.

The weanling should be thoroughly familiarised with the situation of the handler standing near the position shown in colour photo 13. The calm and reassuring handling of the head is of utmost importance in creating a psychological as well as a physical communication with the youngster. The horse must gain enough confidence in the handler to face him, whenever he is approached to be secured. Although this association with the head, while he is tied up, may not convince the horse that the trainer is stronger than the horse, the horse will become aware that the trainer is in control of the situation.

In quite a number of experiments it was observed that the horse could often distinguish between being tied to an immovable object and being held by hand next to the immovable object.

The tie-up rope must not be pulled or jagged to encourage the horse to pull back or fight the restraint. He must be allowed to work it out for himself that when he stops pulling and does not object to the restraint he is allowed peace.

The horse's method of learning through the association of ideas represents a problem when he has to learn to stand at rest while tied to a substantial object in a certain place. He has to learn that when he is in this position and place he is prevented from any degree of flight. The panic and struggle that a horse often shows when he is first tied is quite understandable when it is considered that flight is his main instinct of self-preservation.

Most horses will eventually succumb to the idea that when they are in a certain position in a certain place flight is not possible, but the problem arises that when the horse is tied up to another object in another place the association of ideas is not complete and he will attempt flight. It is necessary, therefore, for the horse to become aware, through an intensity of impression, that it is the restraint that is on or connected to him — such as a rope, rein,

etc. — that is the restraining influence, not necessarily the object to which it is connected or the place in which the horse is situated.

To accomplish this awareness of restraint, and to increase the intensity of impression towards the restraint itself, positive leading and lungeing lessons — immediately following and interspersed with tie-up lessons — are quite a successful procedure.

Sometimes a horse will lie down when first tied up, or even when a girth is fastened. No hitting of the animal is necessary in order to persuade him to stand. The nostrils of the horse are simply pinched together between the thumb and forefinger, cutting off air for a few moments. He will then regain his feet quickly.

A weanling or horse of any age that persistently lies down when given a tie-up lesson, or one that fights in an extremely violent manner when tied up, will learn with the following method.

Approach a young horse with the *back* of the hand extended for the first contact.

The horse is first tied up. As soon as he has had one vigorous pull, or struggle, he is released from the rail. The release must be timed so that he is not actually struggling when he is made aware of being released. The horse is then lunged. He may not be familiar with the lungeing procedure at this stage but as long as he goes around on a loose rein, or rope, and perhaps encouraged by the use of the lungeing whip, it is all that is required.

After three or four lungeing circles he is then re-tied. After another pull or struggle he is again released, and again the timing of awareness of release must be taken when he is accepting the restraint, even if only for a moment. The lungeing is then repeated.

This procedure may have to be repeated a number of times each day over a period of days in extreme cases, but the results show that almost every horse will accept being tied, and the risk of injury is reduced to a minimum.

On condition that he is in a suitable enclosure a weanling can be taught to lunge correctly and respond to a lunge rein and verbal aids; this early introduction to the lungeing procedure will ensure a willingness to lunge later in the horse's life. This is only a lesson to learn the procedure and is not meant to force the horse to exert himself unduly.

When the horse in his first lesson has shown a reasonable acceptance of being tied up, not necessarily a complete acceptance, he is released from the rail. As mentioned earlier, the timing of the horse's awareness of his release is most important.

On release from the tie-up rail the horse is then led around the sand ring or yard, with the harness strap still in place. This will help to instil forward movement and he will become familiar with harness being in place on his body, particularly the strap above his hocks. An assistant walking behind him—out of kicking range, of course—is an advantage with a reluctant leader.

At all times the progress and pause method is used at a practical level. The person leading must use the same position as when the weanling was tied to the rail, i.e. in front and to the side of the horse. The young horse will then willingly lead back to his box, where the gear is removed, he is given a rewarding rub, and he is released to feed and relax.

The tail rope is a popular and very successful alternative aid to forward movement with led horses of all ages. This is a rein or rope fixed as in colour photo 17. The end may be held free, or passed through the headstall or bit ring.

The following day the tie-up procedure is repeated, except that the coacher need not be used, and it is remarkable how the young horse will accept being led almost without question. The tie-up harness can now be dispensed with, and the next three or four days are devoted to just leading the youngster around the stud or farm once or twice each day. When a number of foals are weaned at the same time, it is a good custom to take them out in single file. If the youngster is to be shown in weanling classes or to be presented in a sale ring the horse can be taught to lead from the near-side shoulder as with yearlings.

When these tie-up procedures are followed the percentage of horses not allowing themselves to be tied up is minimal; so, too, is the risk of injury during the tie-up lesson.

The weanling can now be led to a small paddock, or yard, during the day and turned loose to exercise and play, preferably with another weanling companion or companions, and led in again after a few hours (see photo 17). Horses are by nature herd creatures, and also creatures of habit, and it must be remembered not to overdo the love and attention to the extent where they are being treated like hothouse plants.

17.   A short strap approximately 15 cm long is attached to the headcollar ring of the weanling as it is easier to grasp the loose strap than to get hold of a headcollar which is a snug fit against the youngster's head. If a weanling moves just as the fingers are about to grasp the headcollar, the fingers more often than not poke into the weanling's head causing him to duck away, and thus some become frightened of an approaching hand

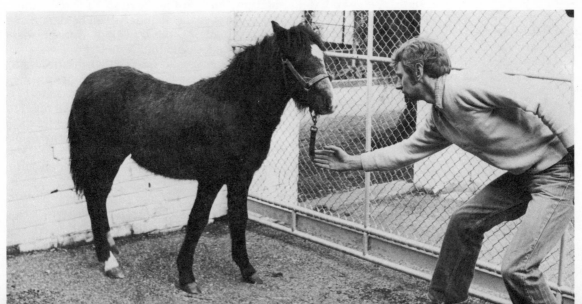

## RUGGING THE WEANLING

A small rug can be introduced and carefully fitted to the youngster at the weanling age, if required. However, it must be in the confines of a horse box or similar enclosure. The youngster should not be turned loose in a big yard or paddock before he has become fully accustomed to the rug. There is an extreme risk that he will panic and gallop into a fence, or that the rug might slip and make him gallop in fear and thereby cause injury to himself.

## TRANSPORTING

Provided that a suitable vehicle is available it is well worth loading the weanling on to a float, or horse transport, and taking him for a journey. It is easier to acquaint him with transport at this age and, as a consequence, he will present fewer problems when older.

When transporting young horses for the first time in a float that has provisions for tying up, the horse is best tied with the neck bag and rope, or a rope as in sketch D, as this may save broken headcollars or leads should the youngster decide to question the procedure.

If transporting young horses in a single or

Sketch D
A non-slip neck rope tie

double horse float towed by a car or truck, it is a good policy to drill a hole in the side or front of the float adjacent to the tie-up ring. The rope can then be wrapped once around the ring and passed through the wall of the float and secured to a ring on the chassis on the outside. Should the horse react in a violent manner necessitating his release, this method of securing eliminates the dangerous situation of a person having to enter the cramped interior of the float in order to effect a release.

A very successful method of transporting weanlings, particularly when there is a considerable number, is to adjust the divisions on a horse transport so that the individual spaces are dispensed with and thus make the area large enough to accommodate two, three, or four weanlings in the one space. The weanlings are turned loose in this space and allowed free movement. This method is very successful in conditioning young horses to travelling.

If the mare and foal should have to be transported before the foal is weaned the early education of the foal is of great value. The foal can be led on to the float in advance of, or accompanied by, his dam if the foal is uneducated, but if there is a safe and well-constructed loading ramp and enclosure available the foal can be encouraged to accompany his dam as she walks on.

Safe loading ramps are often conspicuous by their absence on otherwise well-appointed breeding or training establishments. This should not be so, because the loading ramp is extremely valuable for the introduction of young horses to a transport vehicle. If a mare and uneducated foal have to be loaded and a ramp is not available the foal can be caught and placed bodily on the transport with the mare following close behind.

It is important to ensure that the floor surface of the horse transport used for conveying young horses (or any horses for that matter) is not slippery or in a condition that will prevent the horse from obtaining a secure foothold.

By this stage the weanling is dewormed, his feet are attended to, he is branded if necessary, and he is now ready for the next step in his life.

# 4
# The Yearling

## EDUCATION OF THE YEARLING

If the weanling has been returned to the paddock to be allowed to grow and mature, by the time he is fourteen months old—or a yearling as he is now called— it is a tremendous advantage to the horse, and to all who are associated with him, if his education is further advanced, particularly if he is to be used for speed, or for any purpose calling for grace, suppleness, and fluidity of movement.

The horse is domiciled in his box or similar abode, and the everyday chores of feeding, watering, and general care are intensified with the additional tasks of grooming, rugging, and cleaning out and oiling feet. The best results are achieved if lungeing, more leading lessons, and even hosing down or washing are done slowly at first, and for a short period, and then advanced until they are accepted by the yearling as normal procedure.

When grooming the horse it is advisable to continue from where he was rubbed down with the cloth, as a weanling, and gradually accustom him to a soft brush. Because his coat may look rough or dirty it is not recommended to introduce a hard or stiff brush immediately, as this will tend to irritate him and cause soreness and a resentment of grooming which can result in the trainer or assistant being bitten or kicked.

## RUGGING A YEARLING

Rugging a yearling for the first few times can be a frightening experience for the horse, and hazardous to the trainer if a few basic steps are not adhered too. The rug should be rolled, or folded, in such a manner that it can be placed on the wither and then unrolled, or unfolded, slowly along the back of the horse while he is being held by an assistant. A rug with a surcingle should not be used at this stage, as this could induce bucking and other uncalled-for antics.

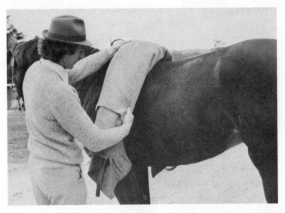

28.   Fitting a rug. The rug can be rolled or folded from the tail end towards the wither, and before placement on the horse. The folded rug is then placed over the horse's wither

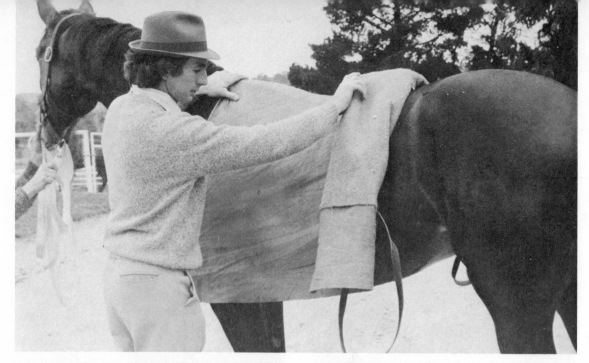

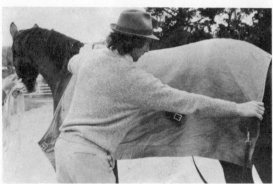

29.  *Top:* The rug is unrolled along the horse's back, with one hand holding it in place at the wither.   30. *Above, left:* The rug is checked for size and fit.   31. *Above, right:* When fastening a rug it is a matter for conjecture whether the front strap or the rear straps should be secured first. There is a theory that should the horse take fright and gallop off with the front portion half secured the rug will slip around the horse's neck and under his feet, whereas if the hind straps are secured first and the horse gallops off then the rug will slip over the rear. The answer is to place the young horse in a confined position where he cannot gallop off

With a horse that is obviously nervous and highly strung, it is best to introduce the rug with the horse's attention diverted to a certain extent by the application of a nose twitch. There are two main types of rug fastening, the 'Y' fittings and the rear leg straps. The rear leg straps, or 'N.Z.' fitting, is preferable, as this type is less likely to slip down one side of the horse provided that both straps are adjusted to the same length.

As with the foal, it is unwise to turn the youngster, inexperienced with a rug, loose in a big yard or paddock until he has become thoroughly accustomed to it.

## LUNGEING

Lungeing is one of the finest exercises that can be given to a horse to develop his suppleness and muscle tone and which, when carried out

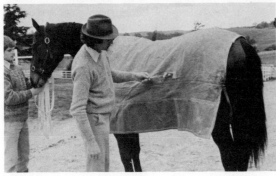

32. *Top:* Adjustment of the rear leg straps is very important. The straps must be exactly the same length so as to balance the rug. They should be comfortable for the horse to wear and be not so tight as to cause pinching or chafing. The straps should also be interlocked with each other where they pass between the horse's hind legs

33. *Above:* This strap and buckle fitting is a very easy one for the horse to unfasten by tugging or chewing on the strap end. A knot tied around the buckle, or the strap passed back through the buckle, will prevent this happening and avert a damaged rug or an injured horse that has been panicked by the partial dislodgement of the rug. The strap end of the front fastening should also be made similarly secure

correctly, will develop a rapport and communication between horse and trainer that can be quite intense and mutually enjoyable.

The most suitable place for lungeing is in a round yard or sand roll approximately 12 m in diameter, but any type of yard is better than open space or a large paddock. The lungeing rein, of webbing or similar material, is attached to the headcollar, training cavesson, or bridle. Remember that a headcollar is simplest; while a training cavesson can have advantages it is not always essential. If a bridle is used one has to be careful not to partially mouth the youngster, which can result in a poor response to the bit when he is finally educated.

## RING, OR TATTERSALL, BIT

The ideal head piece for lungeing a young horse is an ordinary headcollar and ring bit as shown in sketch E. For a yearling's or two year old's first lungeing lesson and first leading lesson the advantages of using this Tattersall, or ring, bit together with a headcollar are that the bit only comes into action when the horse has to be restrained from over-exuberance or unwanted forward movement—even then only a proportion of the pressure is applied through the noseband on the headcollar. Younger horses seem to accept this bit extremely well, and it is easy to enter it into the mouth.

There is no pressure or pulling on the mouth, when the horse is being led from the forward position. This bit does not affect the mouth to the extent that it can become

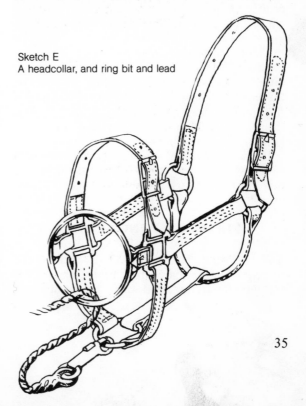

Sketch E
A headcollar, and ring bit and lead

35

unresponsive to future conditioning for answering controls. It also has the added advantage of discouraging the horse from the habit of putting his tongue over the bit.

Horses are creatures of habit and learn by repetition, and if the lungeing procedure is carried out regularly in the following manner excellent results will be obtained.

'The horse is always led to the centre of the ring to commence the exercise. Starting in a clockwise direction, so that the trainer is on the off side, the horse is led around in gradually widening circles. The use of a lungeing whip as an aid to forward movement is a distinct advantage.

The whip is most effective in assisting to gain forward movement when it is brought into contact with the rear of the gaskin area and is to be regarded as an extension of a trainer's arm, to direct and encourage, not as an instrument of torture. The same applies to the use of ropes, bits, riding whips, lungeing whips, catching hooks, etc.

An extreme being the case of a newly-married couple on leaving the church in a horse-drawn carriage. The horse baulked suddenly and refused to go. The husband said, 'That's once', then alighted from the carriage and proceeded to give the horse a hiding with his whip. They then drove on for another kilometre.

The horse baulked a second time. The husband said, 'That's twice', and again alighted to give the horse a second hiding. They continued their journey until the horse baulked a third time. This time the husband said, 'That's thrice', alighted from the carriage, drew his gun, and shot the horse.

His wife, shocked by this harsh treatment, severely reprimanded her husband. When she had finished he turned to her and said, 'That's once'.

## FIRST LUNGEING LESSON

The youngster is led around in a clockwise direction approximately four times. The size of the initial circles need only be small, not necessarily to the full perimeter of the yard.

The handler actually leads the horse from the off side. Should the horse show reluctance, and unfamiliarity at being led from this side, an assistant signalling forward movement by touching the gaskins with a lungeing whip will simplify the procedure. Once progress is made to this extent the horse is led back to the centre of the yard and a pause is effected as a reward.

Verbal, or any other signals that the horse is to learn in relation to the lungeing exercise should begin at this very first lesson.

After the pause in the centre of the yard the lesson is repeated, this time on the near side, or anti-clockwise. Again at completion the horse is led to the centre and a pause effected.

Once the horse is familiar with this basic circling the amount of lunge rein between horse and handler can be increased progressively until the required radius of the circle is achieved.

The horse can be taught to increase the size of the circle by signals, such as the pointing of the lunge whip to his shoulder area, or touching him there.

The method of commencing the lungeing lessons on the off side will combat the reluctance of some animals to work in this manner if they have had very little handling on that side, and/or are extremely familiar with being led from the near side.

When commencing with a young horse it is unwise to give him too much work, thus making him overtired and inattentive; half a dozen laps daily, repeated about three times each way, is quite sufficient for the first few days. To effect a halt while the horse is lungeing, a slight but definite tug on the lungeing rein accompanied by the usual command to halt, and the positioning of the trainer's body towards the horse's line of progress, is very effective.

After the horse has been brought to a halt he is then taught to walk up to the person working him. If he will not do so when pressure is applied to him via the lungeing rein a compromise must be reached, by walking up to the

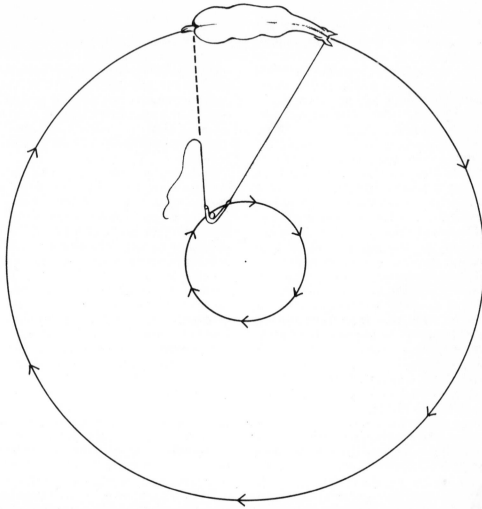

Sketch F
The lungeing procedure is made easier for the horse to comprehend if, during the basic lessons, the trainer is more in line with the horse's hindquarters than with his forequarters. The trainer walking in a circle as shown will also assist the fluidity of these basic lessons. When a halt is required the trainer assumes a position more towards the forequarters

horse and leading him into the centre of the exercise area, or using the method described for weanlings, i.e. causing him to become off balance and thereby produce a step sideways.

The main point is to reassure the horse, and to convince him that where you want him to stand is a good place for him to be and is the place where he receives peace from the trainer's demands.

Repetition of these procedures every day will soon have the horse coming to the centre of the exercise area on command. The horse is then allowed to stand and rest for a few moments, which acts as his reward, before being sent out to lunge in the opposite direction.

If the horse shows hesitation in forward movement during the initial circles of the enclosure he should be encouraged quite definitely by the lungeing whip (sketch F).

These first circling exercises, right and left handed, are vital in the pupil's future willingness to lunge.

Although the progress and pause method should be used to obtain maximum results, any negative behaviour by the trainer at this stage will encourage the horse to take the initiative and assume control of the manoeuvre.

Even though the walk is favoured as the pace to commence lungeing, insistence on the walk only can lead to the horse becoming confused as to what is required of him, to stop or to go. The trot is often more successful.

The failure of young horses to lunge satisfactorily is in most cases due to an inexperienced trainer. The main causes of mistakes are the failure to show and direct the horse, and the lack of a positive approach.

A common fault of a trainer is that of positioning his body too far in front of the horse's line of progress, thereby causing the horse to stop and become confused as to what is required of him.

Lungeing for too long a period, without a pause being effected as a reward, will often force the horse into error.

By using the trot as the main working gait it will become possible to educate the horse over a period of time (governed by the trainer's ability, and the horse's willingness) to walk, trot, or canter at a given command. During these initial lungeing exercises the trainer should be on the alert continually for any lameness that has not been previously evident, and/or any peculiarities in the horse's gait such as cutting or brushing, or the irregular or over-exuberant movement of one leg causing damage or interference to another leg.

The most common occurrence of this nature in young horses is that of the front of the hind foot striking the rear of the front foot, usually known as over-reaching. A very painful wound, plus a deep and severe bruising of the bulbs of the heel, can result from this.

Rubber bell boots fitted over the fore feet can often be of great assistance as a protection, plus a rounding off of the hind hoof and the removal of any cutting edge. A consultation with the farrier is advisable.

Protective leather boots, shin boots, fetlock boots, etc., may supply protection in some instances, but often the addition of the boots' added weight to the legs of a young horse can add to the cause, rather than act as the cure.

## LUNGEING AT LIBERTY

Should the trainer so desire, the lungeing rein can be disconnected from the horse and the horse trained to lunge at liberty. This entails the trainer exercising his control purely by verbal commands, and the positioning of his body in relation to that of the horse.

It is possible to control the horse at liberty through transitions of the walk, trot, and canter (see colour photo 16). This type of exercise is not essential but is extremely beneficial to the trainer in practising the projection of verbal aids, and in the development of a rapport between himself and his pupil. It will also encourage the horse to look to the trainer for his instructions.

To commence lungeing at liberty the horse must first be taught to lunge under complete control while on the lunge rein. Then while the lunge rein is still connected, but slack, the verbal commands are used together with the positioning of the trainer's body and reinforced with arm and hand motions (or lunge whip).

The lunge rein is used in this instance only to correct the horse or to reinforce control. Once the horse will lunge in the enclosure on a slack rein then the rein can be disconnected and the horse lunged at liberty for one short period only — with the trainer simulating the exact positions and signals as with the rein, even to holding the rein coiled as usual in the hand. After one short lesson the rein is reconnected and the horse lunged with the rein.

The sessions at liberty gradually can extend over a number of days as the horse and trainer grow confident of the rapport forming between them.

# 5

# Aids, Mouthing, and Bits

## VERBAL AIDS

The use of verbal aids is a great advantage as a medium during the progress to conventional silent aids—such as reins, leg aids, etc. The trainer should project the word of command to the horse in such a manner that he virtually demands the horse's attention. Bear in mind that it is far easier for the horse to learn a short word of command than a long drawn out sentence.

Words such as walk, trot, canter, steady, easy, whoa, stand, are verbal commands that most horses will learn quite readily on the lunge, as long as there is no great amount of talk coupled with them to confuse the meaning. When success is gained it is often through the tone in which the word is projected more than the actual word itself, and persistent repetition is essential.

Quite a large number of reasonably intelligent horses will eventually respond if desired, to purely verbal commands. A fine sense of achievement can be obtained if a horse's lungeing ability is advanced to this stage.

Once the horse is reasonably educated in the procedure of lungeing, the amount of work should be governed by the condition of the horse and what is required of him, i.e. if he is being prepared for sale, for show, or furthering his education. Whatever the reason, the combination of daily lungeing, of grooming and rugging—combined with sensible feeding, general care of the feet, and control of parasites—will produce a youngster of fine well-being, exceptional muscle tone, and an appearance governed only by his natural conformation.

The decision to continue the horse's education to riding standard is dependent upon his age and maturity. It is recommended that the horse be at least twenty-four months old for racehorses of sprinting bloodlines, and three years of age for ponies, hacks, and staying-bred racehorses.

> Never *underestimate* the ability of a horse to act or react in an extremely violent manner. It is possible for a horse to kick, strike, or bite faster than the human eye can follow the movement.

*X-ray of the radius (forearm) bone directly above the knee as a guide to bone maturity.*

The degree of closure of the distal radial epiphysis is now accepted as a reasonable guide toward bone maturity in horses and may be used as an aid in determining the age at which a horse can commence a training programme

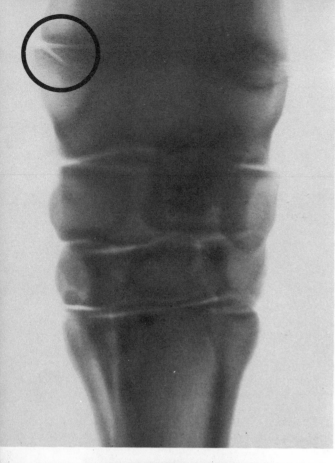

that involves a considerable amount of work and load carrying. If a horse has a closed epiphysial line but is obviously immature and underdeveloped in other aspects, then these other aspects must receive prime consideration. However, the degree of epiphysial closure is a valuable guide in otherwise well-grown horses that look well developed and robust in size but their bone growth may be immature and intense training could result in injury.

## THE MOUTH

Because of the angulation of the crowns of the premolar and molar teeth, the up-and-down movement of the lower jaw produces a shearing action on the food during mastication. The width of the lower jaw, being narrower than the top jaw, also produces an oval to-and-fro action.

Sketch G shows front-to-rear opposing forces of the cheek teeth and the way in which the teeth wear and produce sharp points along the outside of the upper cheek teeth and inside the lower cheek teeth. The points on the upper cheek teeth cause irritations and ulcerations to the inside of the cheeks, particularly when pressure is applied to the bit. The points on the inside of the lower cheek teeth can cause similar damage to the lateral surface of the tongue. A horse's teeth continue to grow throughout his lifetime; this continued growth coupled with an incomplete grinding action can produce very sharp points.

Symptoms of a horse suffering from the above conditions of the mouth are: wads of chewed food left in feed bin; excess mouthing of the bit, resulting in frothing of the lips; a tendency to lug to one side or the other when being driven or ridden; or a tendency to reef and cross jaws, also when being driven or ridden.

Any horse that does not eat well or is in poor

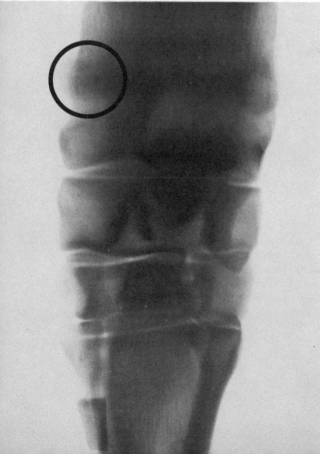

34.   *Top, left:* A radiograph (X-ray) showing partially open epiphyses

35.   *Left:* Another radiograph (X-ray) of closed epiphyses

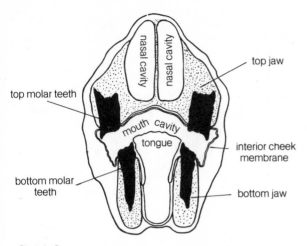

Sketch G
Front to rear opposing forces of cheek teeth showing how the teeth wear and produce sharp points along the outside of the upper cheek teeth, and inside the lower cheek teeth

condition should have his mouth checked for abnormalities and irritations, and any sharp points should be removed by a veterinary surgeon, or a person competent with a tooth rasp.

The first premolar or wolf teeth can sometimes be a source of annoyance. These teeth erupt at from five to six months, and are frequently shed at thirty months, but in many cases they are retained. The general concensus of opinion is that if the teeth are sound, and tight in the gum, they may cause a little trouble, but if they are loose, particularly once the horse has attained the age of thirty months, the teeth are best removed by a veterinary surgeon, or a horse dentist.

A critical stage in the development of the young horse is mouthing and riding for the first time. Like the tying-up procedure the mouthing of horses has been done and part done in so many ways that it is impossible to describe all of them. However, the method detailed here is a good and reliable base for any horse or pony.

It is of the utmost importance that the horse must fully accept the bit being in place in his mouth before any use of the bit as a means of communication or control is attempted. If a

horse is to be taught to respond but has never had a bit in his mouth before then one should be fitted and left on him for short periods (fifteen minutes) at rest, or during lungeing exercise with the lunge rein attached to the headcollar or cavesson, until the horse has fully accepted the bit.

A light but strong bridle is fitted over the normal headcollar. It is advisable to leave the headcollar on the horse so that if the bridle becomes displaced a means of control still exists. Remember, too, that the horse is often unaccustomed to being led from a rein or lead attached to the bit ring.

The horse is then lunged as he has been trained to do, but the lungeing rein is attached to the bit ring. Slight pressure is exerted periodically on the rein as the horse is lungeing, so that he will receive the initial feel of the bit pressure on the bars of his mouth and the corners of his lips. This is the beginning of what is known as the 'open rein'.

The bit used for mouthing (sketch H) should be adjusted so that it is quite firm in the side of the youngster's mouth. A good guide is to adjust so that the corners of the mouth just crinkle, making sure that the bridle is adjusted evenly both sides. The bit must not dangle in the horse's mouth and become a plaything, as this will lead to lack of response and the bad habit of getting the tongue over the bit. This habit is extremely dangerous in racehorses because loss of control and damage to the membrane under the tongue can result.

If a horse should show signs of developing the habit of placing his tongue over the bit a jointed snaffle bit left on the horse over a period of one or two days, while he adjusts to drinking and eating with the bit in place, will usually nip the habit in the bud. (If a bit is left on a horse in this manner hay should not be fed as it will wind around the bit. Chaff and easily masticated feeds are advisable.) Care must be taken to ensure that the corners of the mouth do not become chafed and that the horse is in an area free from objects that can be caught in the big rings.

A major cause of the tongue-over-the-bit

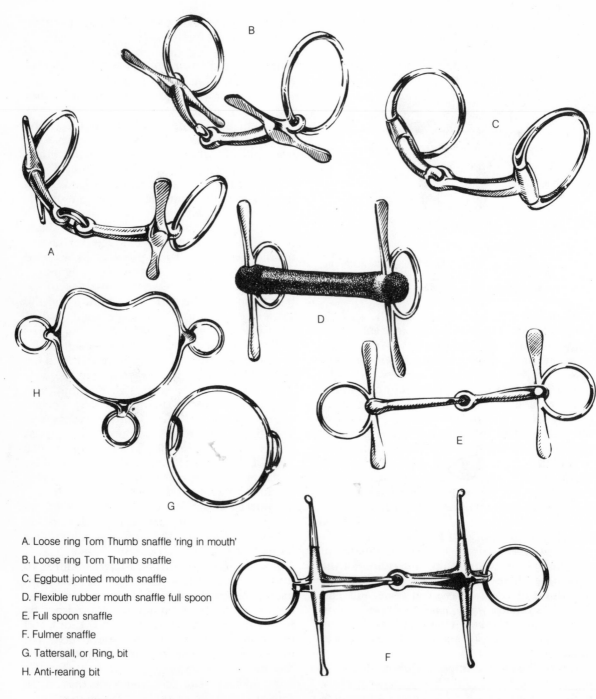

A. Loose ring Tom Thumb snaffle 'ring in mouth'

B. Loose ring Tom Thumb snaffle

C. Eggbutt jointed mouth snaffle

D. Flexible rubber mouth snaffle full spoon

E. Full spoon snaffle

F. Fulmer snaffle

G. Tattersall, or Ring, bit

H. Anti-rearing bit

Sketch H
Various types of bits recommended for mouthing. Anti-rearing and Tattersall bits are not used for mouthing

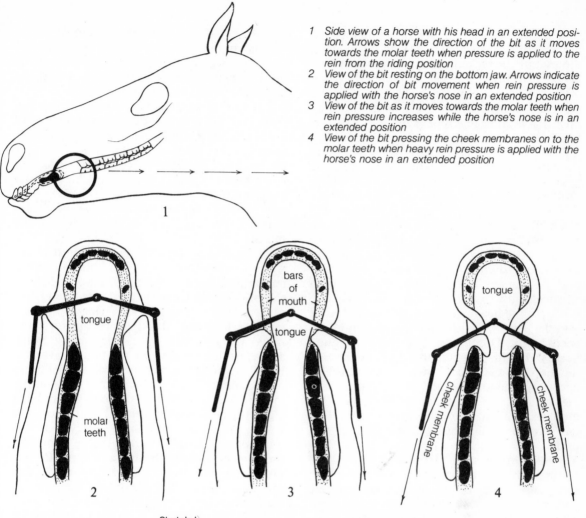

1 Side view of a horse with his head in an extended position. Arrows show the direction of the bit as it moves towards the molar teeth when pressure is applied to the rein from the riding position
2 View of the bit resting on the bottom jaw. Arrows indicate the direction of bit movement when rein pressure is applied with the horse's nose in an extended position
3 View of the bit as it moves towards the molar teeth when rein pressure increases while the horse's nose is in an extended position
4 View of the bit pressing the cheek membranes on to the molar teeth when heavy rein pressure is applied with the horse's nose in an extended position

Sketch I
When excess rein pressure is applied to horse's mouth

habit during basic education is excess pressure being applied to the horse's mouth from the bit, causing the horse to be frightened of keeping his tongue in the correct position for fear of its being hurt by a jerk of the bit (see sketch I).

## FITTING THE BRIDLE

Correct fitting of the bridle is very important. The light but strong bridle is fitted making sure that it is comfortable for the horse to wear. The top headstrap behind the ears should be free of tangled mane and doubled pieces of forelock and the headstrap and forehead band should not rest against, or interfere with the ears of the horse once the bridle is in position. The throat strap should be adjusted so that, no matter how the horse's head is turned or flexed, it never causes a restriction or becomes tight. The cheek straps should be even on both sides.

43

A bridle that has plenty of adjustment is preferable to one which has fixed headpieces. Straps must be tucked neatly and securely into keepers: if these are left flapping they can often be a source of irritation to a young horse and cause him to throw his head about in an undesirable and dangerous manner in an effort to be rid of the annoyance.

A horse that is particularly touchy around the ears, and will not allow the headpiece to be passed over them, can be educated to accept bridling by using the following method.

The nose twitch is applied, which will restrain the horse's head from violent movement (see colour photo 25). The headstrap is then passed slowly over the ears by a person tall enough to do so without having to try and pull the horse's head downward. It is often advantageous to remove the bit from the bridle, fit the headpiece, and then enter the bit into the pupil's mouth and rebuckle on to the cheek straps. Do not forget to open the young horse's mouth, to enter the bit, by inserting the thumb in the side of the mouth; this is also necessary when the bridle is being removed as the horse does not automatically open his mouth and allow the bit to drop out until he has become familiarised with the removal of a bridle.

If this procedure is carried out daily it will be found that the twitch can be dispensed with eventually: the muzzle is then held tightly by one hand, simulating the twitch position, while the headpiece is fitted. This is accomplished with a number of lessons over the period of time necessary for the horse to accept the procedure. The next step is to *place* the hand on the muzzle for a number of lessons, then on the nose for a number of lessons, and then to fitting the bridle normally.

This is a very successful method, particularly with horses that are violent with their refusal to have their ears touched, and it is far safer and quicker than wrestling and being dragged around a box or yard with one hand in the air trying to reach a frantic horse's ears and poll area.

It is all very well to try and induce a horse to accept a person's hand rubbing around his ears if he is not too violent in his reactions, but it is just a source of annoyance if he throws his head up high to a position where it is virtually impossible to reach the poll.

The snaffle bit should be adjusted so that the corners of the mouth, or junction of upper and lower lips, just crinkle, resulting from the bit's contact. The width of the bit is important. If the bit is too wide it will give a false impression when being adjusted as the rings held by the cheekstraps will hold the ends of the bit in the corners of the mouth but will leave the excess length forming a deep 'V' inside the horse's mouth.

All this spare and unwanted length of bit within the horse's mouth not only will lessen constant, even contact but also will heighten the risk of a sudden, jarring contact, and also cause a sawing action when changes of direction are indicated through pressures via the reins. The enlarged 'V' also leaves too much scope for the horse to put his tongue over the bit. If the bit is too narrow it will virtually jam on the horse's jaws, pressing the tissue on the inside of the mouth on to the teeth and causing a great deal of discomfort and distraction.

The traditional mouthing bit, which has 'players' or 'keys' attached to the centre in order to encourage the horse to 'mouth' the bit, is questionable in its efficiency. It can often encourage a horse in the undesirable habit of excess playing with the bit.

A side bar jointed snaffle with a reasonably thick mouthpiece is generally a good bit for initial mouthing, providing the ends of the side bars are wide or bevelled off above the mouthpiece when fitted, to allow for the widening of the horse's head. Although an egg butt bit or a cheek ring jointed snaffle bit, is sometimes satisfactory, side bars will prevent the bit from sliding through the mouth.

The cheek ring in particular can actually encourage or lever the horse's mouth open with a prising action when pressure is applied through the corresponding ring.

The thickness and construction of horses' lips vary with every individual and must be considered when fitting and adjusting the bit for mouthing. The joining point of upper and lower lips can vary in the distance between this joining point and the cheek tooth, therefore the bit should be adjusted to each horse's mouth depending on these distances.

## FITTING THE ROLLER

The next piece of harness to be applied is the roller, or continuous girth. This is best done as in colour photo 22. The horse is held by an assistant, and the roller applied by passing it from the trainer's shoulders over the youngster's wither as in colour photo 23, and then securing it slowly but firmly.

The assistant holding the horse's head makes sure that the horse stands still while this procedure is in progress. When the roller is fitted, the horse is allowed to lunge as usual. Should the horse take exception to the pressure of the girth, which is not uncommon when first it is applied, the methods of disapproval are shown mainly in pig rooting, bucking, and high kicking, while some horses grind their teeth and others switch their tails.

If the preliminary training of lungeing, etc., has been carried out the resistance will be at a minimum and can be limited to a very short space of time. It is far safer for the horse to be geared up and lunged in this manner than to have the gear applied and the horse turned loose in the yard or box. While being lunged he is under control to a certain extent but if turned loose he may panic and crash into the sides of the yard and sustain unnecessary injury.

## SIDE REINS

Side reins can be fitted when the horse has accepted the girth. These are short reins, which are attached to the bit ring or headcollar at one end, and the ring or 'D's, buckle, or terrets on the roller at the other end. The reins should be adjusted at this stage and the horse lunged both ways with the lunge rein attached to the headcollar as in photo 36. He should

then be left in a yard or sand ring for approximately half an hour (with the gear in place) as in photos 37, 38, and 39.

36. *Top:* When lungeing with a side rein fitted, attach the lungeing rein to the headcollar or cavesson, not to the bit ring which causes a two-way pressure on the mouth

37. *Above:* Side reins attached to the headcollar

45

38. *Top:* Side reins attached to the junction of the cheek strap, noseband, and lower cheek strap

39. *Above:* Side reins attached to the bit rings

These photos show three methods of using side reins that can be attached to a cavesson, a headcollar, or the bit rings—depending on requirements and on acceptance by the horse.

Over a series of lessons gradually tighten the side reins evenly on both sides, in order to encourage the horse to flex at the junction of the head and the neck. When the reins are attached to the bit ring a certain amount of give and relaxation of the bottom jaw can be accomplished if the tension of the reins is adjusted with care and feeling for the horse's mouth.

The tension of side reins used in this manner should never be constant: pressure should be brought to bear upon the noseband or bit only when the head is extended.

## THE CRUPPER

Sometimes a young horse is encountered that has very little wither development, causing problems in keeping the saddle from sliding forward on to his neck. A crupper, photo 40, can be employed to prevent this. The strap from the dock to the rear of the saddle, or roller, should be adjusted so that the depth of four fingers can be inserted comfortably between the horse's back and the strap. If a crupper is obviously going to be needed, the best time to introduce it to the horse is when he is at the stage of being lunged with the roller, or the roller and side reins. Some horses object to a crupper under the dock and show their disapproval by kicking, so that great care should be taken when fitting the crupper in the first instance.

## FLEXION

For the horse who is very touchy around the head, or carries his head extremely high or extended, the reins can be attached to the headcollar, or a training cavesson can be substituted and the reins attached to the side rings of the cavesson. Thus in the ensuing lessons he will learn neck flexion, and a flexing at the poll, without undue roughness on the mouth. Once this flexion has been obtained the side reins can be attached to the bit ring. A very successful method of this initial bitting on a big or obviously bold-going young horse is to use a straight bar rubber bit and then change to the jointed snaffle when the turning lessons commence.

Flexion at the poll and neck and lower jaw in small ponies, especially the thickset, chunky type, can be obtained with the use of a roller with a small swivel wheel fixed at the wither position. A piece of sashcord, or similar, is attached to the bit ring, then passed through the swivel wheel as in photo 40. This allows the pony greater movement of the head and neck area and does not cramp his small stature.

There are numerous ways of attempting to obtain this flexion, and the horse's acceptance of the bit. There are methods such as the side reins being attached to the bit ring, then continuing through one or more swivels on the roller and back to the opposite side bit ring. A second method is a short strap connecting the two bit rings under the chin, and through this strap a continuous side rein is passed from one side of the roller to the other.

Yet another method is to connect the bit rings under the chin with a standard martingale type of equipment which is passed between the horse's front legs and secured on to the girth, and so on (sketch J). There are a lot more ingenious ways known best by the trainers who use them. Also there is the chap who tied the bit ring on the horse's bridle back to his tail and stated that 'the more flies there were around, the more he would switch his tail, and the quicker the colt would mouth himself'.

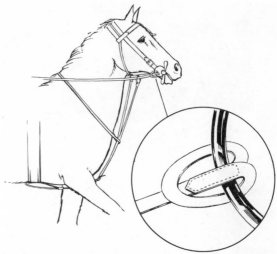

Sketch J
The attachment of reins to the bit ring. This is a good method of attachment for basic education work where the ring of the running martingale cannot be caught up. The use of a rubber grip is optional according to the trainer's preferences and weather conditions. The use of a running martingale is a good policy while riding young horses—the lowered angle of the rein, through the martingale ring if the horse puts his head too high, assists in keeping the bit in position on the bars of the horse's mouth. The passage of the rein through the martingale rings removes portion of the direct pressure from hand to bit

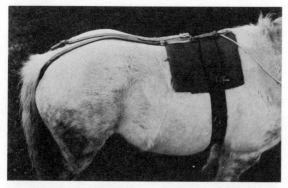

40. A crupper, showing ample room for adjustment and ease of fitting and removal. The photo also shows a roller, or continuous girth. Cord side reins can be seen passing through the swivel wheel—good for initial mouthing of small ponies

The lungeing and half-hour periods in the yard are continued over a number of days, and the side reins are gradually tightened evenly on both sides, so that a little pressure is put on the horse's mouth when he is lunged at the trot until it is obvious that he is beginning to flex at the crest and the junction of his head and neck and to relax his bottom jaw if connected to the bit ring without causing damage or soreness to his mouth, see photo 41.

Although some horses tend to rub the surface skin at the corners of the mouth, due to having very soft or fleshy lips, it is certainly not necessary to purposely make a horse sore in order to mouth him.

Flexion at the poll and neck area and relaxing of the bottom jaw are essential for maximum control over the horse for, when the trainer applies pressure on the bit to steady or halt, the horse with flexion will respond far

41. Over a series of lessons gradually tighten the side reins evenly on both sides in order to encourage the horse to relax his bottom jaw, and also to encourage flexion at the junction of the head and the neck.

The horse must be encouraged to yield to the mere presence of the adjusted gear. There must always be ample room within the adjustment for relief from the inconvenience. The adjustment of the side reins must not attempt to force the horse to submit to pressure

more evenly, and under full control, than a horse with a straight stiff neck and head which results in an almost insurmountable line of resistance. Care must be taken not to cause the horse to overbend the neck and head carriage. This can be regarded as a fault and when excessively overbent can lead to an almost complete loss of control.

Not only has the horse to learn to yield to the presence of a bit when mouthing but also he has to learn to flex and use the muscles in the neck and crest area. This may not present a problem to some horses, but in others the suppleness, flexing, and use of the muscles in conjunction with the signals transmitted through the bit, may take considerable time and training.

The snaffle bit is designed so as to transmit steady and even pressure when required to the corners of the lips and the inside of the horse's lower jaw (the bars). It is not for jagging or using in a violent manner. There is no allowance for give and take in a snaffle bit, it is virtually a 'hot line' in contact with the horse's mouth. The give and take must be in the hands of the person controlling the reins.

Perhaps the biggest fault in the snaffle bit is the manner in which it slides back up the

*Captions for colour photos:*

1. Educating the two-day-old foal to lead alongside his dam.

One handler leads the foal and one handler leads the mare for the first few lessons until the foal responds well enough to enable one handler to lead both mare and foal.

A slip lead is in use here. The lead rein (in this case a piece of baling twine) is not fastened to the foal's headcollar but simply threaded through the ring under the jaw, enabling both ends to be held by the handler. Should a situation arise necessitating the release of the foal the handler releases only one end of the lead rein, allowing it to slip through the headcollar ring and be retained by the handler, thus eliminating the dangerous situation of a young horse running free with a lead rein dragging

2. A safe method of catching the foal—the foal is manoeuvred into a position between the mare and a substantial fence or wall

3. Leading mares and foals between night quarters and day yards where the climatic conditions cause them to be housed at night

4. A previously unhandled foal of considerable size being restrained and controlled by grasping both ears while he is in contact with his dam. In this instance a stomach tube is being inserted through the nostril by a veterinary surgeon

5. A mare about to be led into a pen. The foal is manoeuvred into a smaller pen alongside

6. Mare and foal secure in a double pen with the rear gates closed

7. A previously unhandled foal about to have a headcollar fitted. All sides and ends of the pen are actually gates constructed as top and bottom sections, allowing access to any part of the unhandled foal for close examination, treatment, etc.

8. The gates open to release the mare and foal. The foal is given the opportunity to learn how to manoeuvre through a gate

*Think* first before making an issue out of something the young horse does or does not want to do.

▲1  ▼2

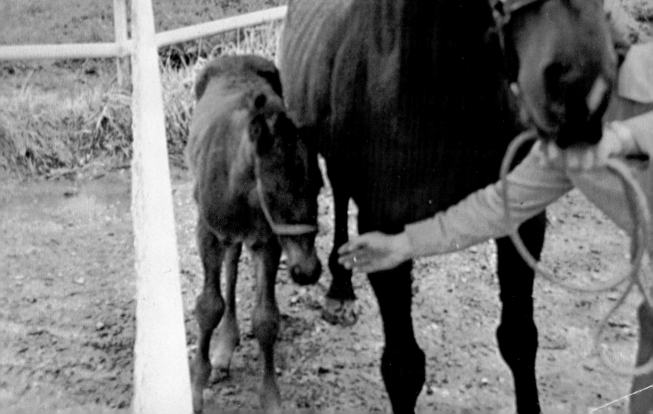

▲3  ▼4                                                                    5 ▶

▲6     ▲7    ▼8

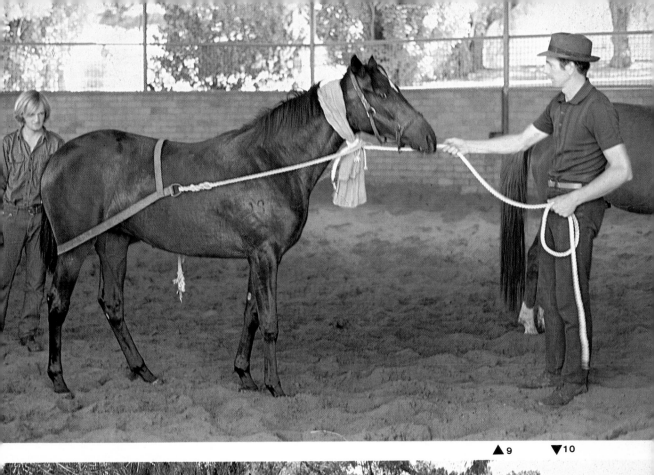

▲9 ▼10

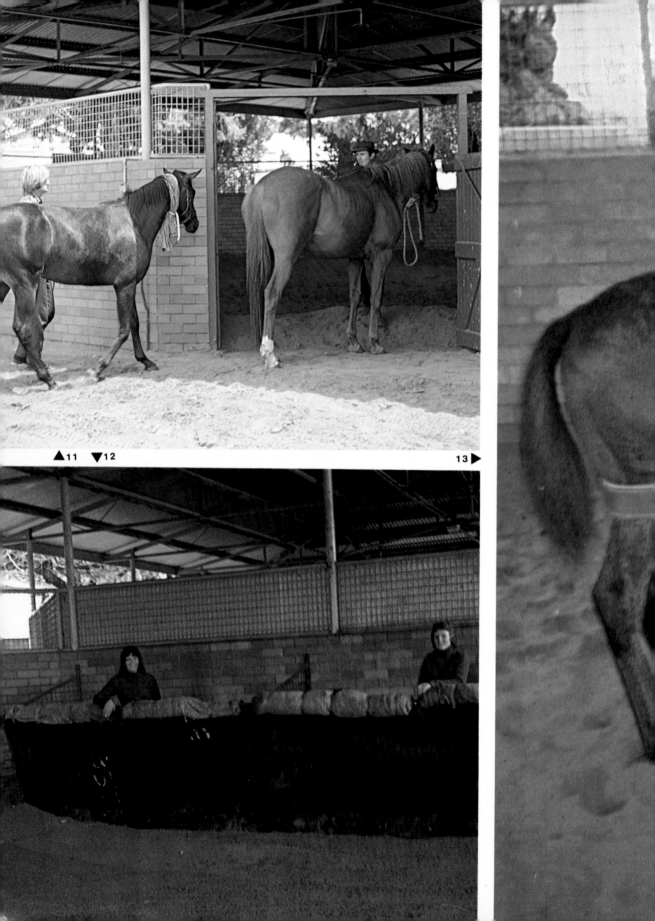

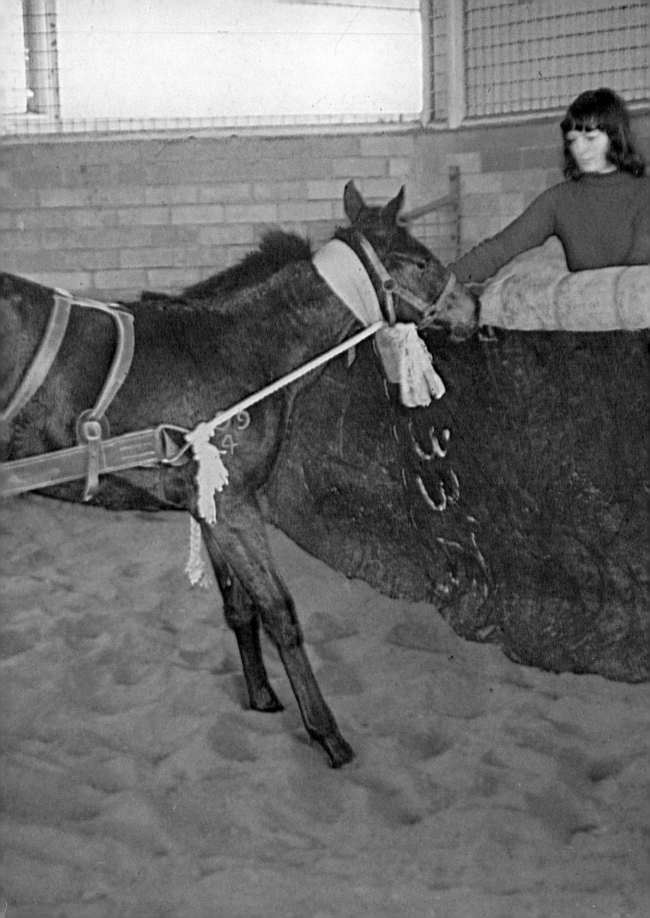

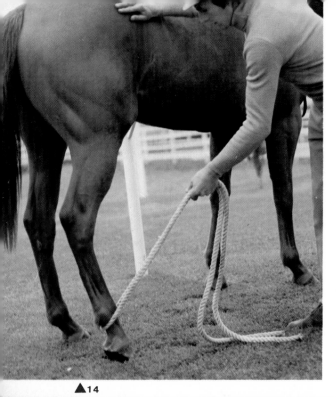
▲14

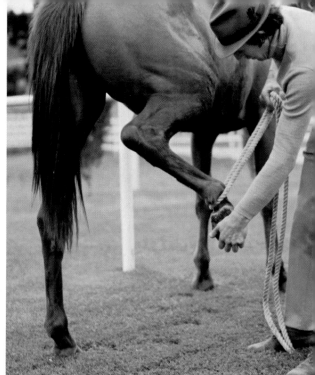
▲15 ▼16

*Captions for colour photos:*

9.  Harness used to assist in educating a weanling to lead or tie up.

The rope from the ring on the leather harness is separate from the lead rope. It passes over the lead rope just below the join of the lead rope and neck bag and is returned to the corresponding ring on the near side of the horse, adjusted, and tied. Adjustment of tension is so that when pressure is applied to the lead rope a proportional amount of pressure is applied to the gaskin via the rear harness strap

10.  The weanling is encouraged to follow the coacher from point to point. Very little if any tension is applied to the lead rope, and the handler positions himself behind the line of the weanling's path

11.  Although all weanlings may not follow the coacher as close as the one demonstrated the general direction can be attained quite successfully

12.  A padded tie-up rail with provision for tieing up two weanlings at any one time. The rail is constructed in such a manner that it is offset from the wall, allowing handlers access between wall and rail.

Rubber padding with chain mesh on the wall side is secured to a top rail (additionally padded) and a bottom rail, which is below the level of the yard surface (sand in this case). The structure is built to accommodate an adult horse in the manner that the horse's head is just over the height of the padded rail. The adjustment for height to accommodate a younger or smaller horse is made by adding or subtracting sand in front of the tie-up rail.

The bottom rail is angled in towards the wall to allow ample room for the horse's forelegs as in colour photo 13

13.  A weanling having a tie-up lesson. The harness is placed in position and, if the weanling takes exception to the harness while having a leading lesson and attempts to displace it or kick, it can be made secure by linking the two rings (or 'D's) on the harness with the excess rope from the knot on the near-side ring (or 'D').

The rope is linked under the girth area behind the forelegs and should not be so tight that it will provoke a weanling to reject the harness but should be tight enough to prevent displacement of the harness.

A guide to the percentage of weanlings that take exception to harness is that only two out of 150 recently tied up in this manner showed any real objection.

It is preferable to have two people handle the weanlings at this stage. One at the weanling's head and the other touching and familiarising him with the hand, brush, saddlecloth, etc.

14.  A simple method of raising the hind foot of a horse that resents the hand being moved in contact down his leg

15.  Although demonstrated here on a yearling this is a very good method to use on weanlings. It enables the foot to be raised and lowered a number of times to teach the weanling to balance, at the same time making work easier for the handler

16.  Her Majesty the Queen, accompanied by Mr C. S. Hayes, watching a demonstration by the author of a horse lungeing at liberty (control by verbal aids and positioning of the trainer's body only). This twenty-month-old thoroughbred colt was trained to lunge without a rein in upward and downward transitions of the walk, trot, and canter and to halt and return to trainer on command. Note the position of the trainer's body in relation to the horse's line of progress

mouth when the nose is held high as in number 1 of sketch I, therefore it is in the interests of the horse that some degree of flexion be obtained at the joining of the head and neck, either before or during his initial mouthing lessons. Thus the bit will stay in position and do the job for which it is designed: to transmit mild pressures from a direct contact with the hands via the reins.

Because the conformation of every horse is different a situation is presented whereby the degree of neck flexion will be different. In some horses the flexion is natural or easy to attain, in others—such as a horse with a long neck and extended head carriage—it is far more difficult. Time and patience are often needed to obtain flexion in ponies with a short, chunky neck.

With racehorses it is far better to ensure flexion for their initial riding stage than to risk the horse trying to exert his natural tendency to extend himself by proceeding with forward movement with his nose held up in the air.

This flexion is also important at the end of a race, or fast workout, when the jockey applies pressure to the bit in order to steady or effect a halt. Damage can be done to a tired horse's legs if he resists the jockey to the extent of throwing his head in the air, and reefing and bounding against the bit. This brings to bear great pressures and strains on tired tendons and ligaments.

# 6
# Training and Driving

## TURNING LESSONS

There is no great advantage in having the roller on the young horse for great lengths of time, e.g. four or five hours. It is far more educational to apply the girth twice a day, and leave it in place for half an hour at this stage. Leaving tight gear, such as rollers, girths, etc., on young horses for long periods is often the cause of girth galls, sores, and skin irritations—particularly if the horse perspires freely and the girths or saddle marks are not entirely cleansed after the gear is removed, as in colour photo 18.

When the horse is lunged with side reins attached to the bit ring, attach the lungeing rein to the headcollar, or cavesson, not to the bit ring.

When flexion at the poll and neck area has been obtained, and the horse has obviously accepted the bit and is relaxing the bottom jaw, he can now progress to some turning lessons. This is achieved by adjusting the side reins so that the off side rein is tighter than the near side, to the extent that the pressure tilts the horse's head just outside the line of his body.

Again this is commenced on the off side. Leave the horse with the gear adjusted for approximately ten minutes in the yard, then adjust the reins so that the near side is tighter, as in colour photo 24, again for approximately ten minutes. Do this twice daily on both sides.

The second day the procedure is carried out as before, except that the tighter rein is shortened one or two holes, and of course the opposite side is slackened off accordingly. By the third day most horses, as soon as the side reins are attached in this manner, will start moving around in circles toward whichever side has the tight rein attached. When the horse does this voluntarily he is ready to drive.

Side reins are preferred if they have a clip at each end with the adjusting buckle in between. It is then a simple matter when giving the horse turning lessons to unclip the reins and change them over, thus giving exactly the same pressure each side. Some reins are available that have an elastic insert to allow a certain amount of give, but these are not necessary.

It is possible to drive the horse without going through the preliminary turning procedure, but a more responsive mouth and greater control are assured if the turning lessons are carried out. It also gives the horse time to learn gradually that when he yields to the pressure that pressure ceases.

Remember, when educating a young horse, to give him a *chance to learn,* don't expect him to *know.*

A funny thing happened at a racing stable when a new young strapper had charge of a horse that wouldn't roll in the sand ring after his track work, but waited until he was returned to his box where he would proceed to roll, and invariably became cast against the wall. The strapper asked the foreman how he could prevent this and the foreman replied 'Show him what to do'. The young strapper was the laugh of the stable when he was discovered rolling around in the sand with his horse gazing in wonderment at him from the side of the roll. But when, as the foreman originally intended, another horse was given a roll in front of the reluctant horse, the latter almost immediately proceeded to enjoy having a good roll in the safety of the sand ring.

The moral of this story has its roots in the fact that the horse is a herd creature and will often follow or copy the actions of his fellows in a similar, and often identical, manner.

Another example is when three horses being ridden side by side on a training track suddenly stopped, almost as one, and threw their riders clean over their heads into a writhing heap on the ground. The cause of this sudden stop had been a piece of paper moving on the side of the track, but the moving paper had been in such a position as to be visible to only one (the outside) horse.

What had happened was that the instinct of the herd by the other horses had overridden all other motivations and they had copied the actions of the shying horse—and copied them so quickly that their combined actions gave the impression that they had all seen the paper.

This instinct of copying other members of his kind can be used to advantage by giving a tardy horse a 'lead' with another, more willing, horse. It can also be a disadvantage when the habits of shying, weaving, windsucking, etc., even bucking, are copied.

## DRIVING, OR LONG REINING

When the horse is ready to be driven for the first time the roller is fitted as usual, but the short side reins are dispensed with and instead a pair of driving reins or two lungeing reins are used. The following method for driving for the

42. Commencement of the driving lesson

first time is very successful and safe. Actually it is a continuation of the lungeing exercises.

The driving reins are passed through the lower 'D's or terrets on the roller, one on the off side and one on the near side. It should be remembered that this procedure is to be accomplished in a suitable, enclosed yard or sand ring.

The horse is now led to the outside perimeter of the enclosure by an assistant while the driver stays near the centre. Similar to the lungeing position, note that the driving rein is not around the hocks of the youngster at this stage but over his back, photo 42. An assistant leading the horse is not only starting the animal off in the right manner, but also it is allowing the driver time to adjust the length of the reins according to the feel of the horse's mouth, and to coil excess rein in the hands.

The assistant releases his hold and the driver takes over control by lungeing the horse in the circular fashion, communicating through both reins via roller terrets (see colour photo 19). Walking and trotting are sufficient paces for the first drive, as long as forward movement under control is obtained. Neck flexion and relaxation of the lower jaw will now become evident. After two or three circles of the enclosure the horse is brought to a halt by applying presssure to the mouth via the reins—accompanied by the usual command to halt—not by pulling back on the reins, but by refusing to allow enough rein for the horse to proceed forward comfortably. If desired the driving reins can be attached to the side rings on a cavesson or headcollar, and control from the bit left to a later date.

The positioning of the trainer in relation to the position of the horse is of great importance. When the horse is asked for forward movement the trainer should position himself more toward the rear of the horse but, when the youngster is asked to halt or turn the trainer should be positioned more in a line toward the horse's forequarters. Once the halt is effected the horse is allowed to pause and stand for a few moments and then commanded to move off again in the same direction.

It is essential that pressure is removed from the reins when the horse responds to that pressure; if the response is momentary, the relief of pressure must be momentary. Gradual awareness by the horse of this peace from pressure will induce him to seek more peace, thus effecting a responsive halt and pause, or rest period. A basic requirement for all riders is, when required, having a horse that can be brought to a halt and wait for further instructions.

## FIRST CHANGE OF DIRECTION

The horse can be induced to turn or change direction after a number of halts have been effected satisfactorily and the trainer is convinced that the horse is aware of what is required of him, so far as that particular lesson is concerned.

Turning is carried out by bringing the horse to a halt in a position far enough away from the boundary fence or wall to enable a turn to be effected in that direction. A pause is allowed and then, by exerting pressure via the rein on the opposite side to which he has been working, the horse is induced to bend his neck and face into the desired direction. The verbal command to walk is then given and, as the horse turns, the corresponding rein is adjusted accordingly to allow the horse to complete the manoeuvre. The horse should be induced to turn and proceed with forward movement as the rein is lifted clear so that the hindquarters pass under it, as in photo 43.

If this rein is allowed to pass around the

43. The horse is brought to a halt, leaving enough space between the horse and the side of the yard to effect a turn

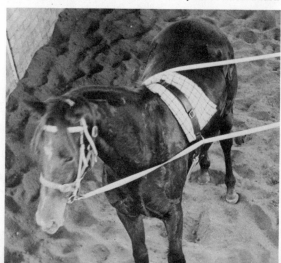

44. As with the rein over the back method the horse is brought to a halt. Pressure is then applied through the offside rein to incline his head and neck

gaskins or hocks of a young, nervous horse, he will often panic and kick. The rein over the back method gives a far more sensitive feel of the mouth.

The rein around the gaskins is a method that is beneficial in engaging a horse's hindquarters and teaching him to bend when turning once he has accepted the contact of the rein in this area—photo 44.

It is safer to drive the horse with this rein over his back, until he is accustomed to the type of work, before allowing the reins to pass around his gaskins. If the preliminary turning lessons have been given as described, the young horse will turn quite willingly without any undue pressure being transmitted through the driving reins to the mouth.

The lessons of halting, followed by a pause, are now repeated, while the horse is working in the opposite direction. When this is being accomplished satisfactorily, the turn or change

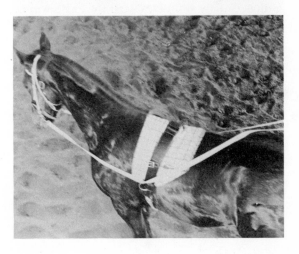

45. *Top, right:* Through the application of pressure to the off side of the horse's mouth the head and neck are inclined toward the open space between the horse and the side of the yard. The rein pressure should not be constant, but more of a give-and-take, gentle, tugging action

46. *Centre, right:* The horse is given the signal for forward movement, and as he turns the opposite rein is lifted upward so that the hindquarters can pass under it

47. *Bottom, right:* The completed turn, with the horse facing the opposite direction. A pause now can be effected or the horse can be signalled to proceed with forward movement

of direction is effected again. The pupil can now be driven either way in the enclosure, stopping and turning periodically, but the amount of work per lesson must not be overdone.

Because it imposes a lot of concentration and a certain amount of collection, the driving procedure is quite demanding of a young horse, and it is now carried out once or twice daily. The horse is taught to walk, trot, and canter on command, halt and turn on command and, gradually, to turning and changes of direction without the preliminary halt, by using pressure and the release of pressure on the appropriate rein or reins.

Once the horse has reached a satisfactory standard of driving under control, the driving rein can be passed through rings or terrets nearer to the horse's wither: this conveys the rein at a comparative angle towards where the rider's hands will be when the youngster is eventually ridden.

As soon as the horse has grasped the basic principles of coming to a halt, and changing direction, the exercise shown in sketch K which calls for more fluidity of movement and response can be practised.

Another method of driving is to harness the horse with the addition of a collar. The driving reins are passed through a ring high up on the side of the collar and then through the high terrets on a roller. Thus the angle of the reins almost exactly simulates what the angle will be when reins are in a rider's hands.

Yet another method of driving is to saddle the horse and tie the stirrup irons together by passing a strap underneath the horse's stomach. The driving reins are then passed through the stirrup irons. This method is only suitable for driving with the trainer positioned behind the horse, and tends to encourage a horse to work with his head lowered or overbent. The flexion is also obtained in the crest closer to the horse's wither than the poll, hence, when he is ridden, the angle of the rein is totally different and the horse often finds it difficult to adjust to the higher point of flexion.

48. *Top:* Due to the rein under pressure touching the offside gaskin the horse will often be influenced into movement by this pressure and not by the trainer's commands

49. *Centre:* The pressure on the offside gaskin and subsequent response can be used to advantage on a horse that is lazy or is very tardy in using his hindquarters

50. *Above:* The completed turn, showing the nearside rein now around the gaskin

However, the overall factor in the positioning of the reins through high, medium, or low

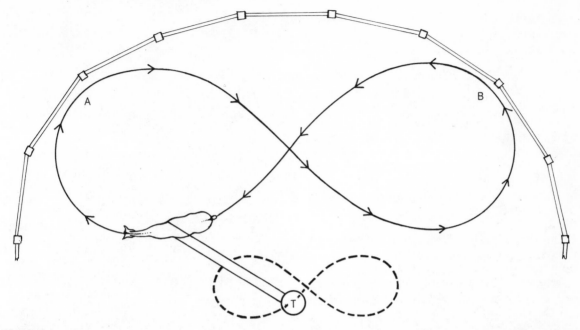

Sketch K
Driving exercise for fluidity of movement and response to the rein-over-back method. The trainer moves in a smaller 'figure of eight' because his arms are extended when the horse attains positions A and B

terrets on the roller is governed by the flexion at the poll and the head carriage of the horse. If the head carriage is too high the reins will need to be positioned through a low 'D' ring or terret. If the head carriage is too low the rein should be positioned through a medium terret, to lift the horse's head up in order to engage it as the controlling factor. Increased impulsion from the hindquarters should be obtained, thus engaging the bit's contact in the mouth more positively.

A drop noseband is an effective piece of equipment for rectifying the fault in horses that evade the bit by opening their mouths continually while being driven or ridden. The horse can also be driven around the property, through stables, laneways, etc., from directly behind. See photo 51.

One of the big advantages, however, of driving the horse in the lungeing manner is that the horse can be driven at speed, trotting, and slow cantering, without the trainer having to break the four-minute mile behind him. If a

51. Driving the horse from behind. When not in an enclosure it is safer during the education period to allow one rein, usually the nearside, to bypass the dee or terret on the roller. This results, as shown, in direct line of control to the head should the horse and/or driver be involved in a situation in which the rein via the roller is ineffective

young horse has been confined to a walk in all of his driving lessons, when he is mounted and proceeding with his lessons under a rider's

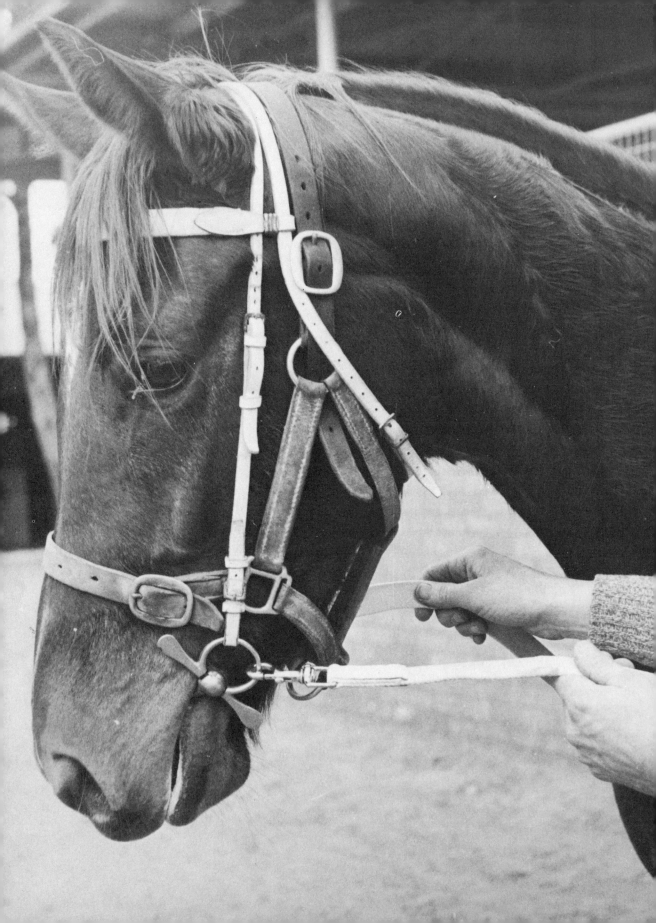

control he will often find it difficult to adjust to the downward transitions from canter to trot and trot to walk, and also to turn at the canter.

It also gives far more confidence to the future rider if he can drive the pupil at the walk, trot, and canter, and bring the horse to a halt from any of these paces.

## THE REIN BACK

The horse can be taught to rein back while still at the driving stage. The method recommended requires an assistant at the horse's head. The horse is brought to a halt and allowed to pause, he is then led forward a step or two by the assistant until he can be induced to stand with his weight distributed on his legs unevenly, in other words not completely balanced but ready to take the next stride. The assistant then applies pressure to the bit via the reins, as in photo 52, accompanied by a command such as 'back', 'back up', etc. With the horse off balance it is relatively easy to effect a first step backwards. Another manner of teaching the rein back is to combine pressure on the nose and shoulder of the horse as in photo 53.

As the horse learns to respond, the trainer in the driving position can take over from the assistant, and control is gradually transferred from the assistant at the horse's head to the trainer in the driving position.

The arm over the back method can also be used to teach a rein back, although the effect of the arm touching the back or wither of the horse can sometimes cause unwanted forward movement.

Ponies and horses of small stature can be driven on short reins with the arm over the back (simulating a driving position—photo 54), provided that the height of the horse allows the trainer's arm to pass over comfortably.

54. Driving on short reins with the arm over the horse's back. The amount of rein back or backing that a young horse is taught in these early stages of his education should be confined to the basic rudiments of the exercise. If he should become overfamiliar with the method of reversing the horse can and will use it as a means of evading forward movement during later parts of his basic education

Another method of teaching the rein back at the driving stage is by facing the horse up to the wall or fence of the exercise ring with the trainer positioned behind the horse's quarters. The command is given for the horse to proceed forward but, as the foreleg is poised in mid stride the trainer checks the movement by refusing to give sufficient rein for the horse to complete the stride, therefore the raised leg has to come back to its original position. This movement can be accompanied by the word 'back', hence 'walk back', with the emphasis and deeper tone of voice on the word 'back'. This is a good basic start to the rein back, which can progress with repetition over a number of days to one step back, two steps back, and so on.

52. *Facing page:* In the initial teaching of rein back the horse is induced to stand a little off balance to enable the trainer to effect a step backwards by exerting pressure to the bars of the mouth

53. *Below:* The combination of pressure on the nose and the shoulder (the horse will yield to these pressures far more willingly if he is initially off balance). The command to be taught, such as 'back' or 'back up', should always be accompanied by the application of pressure and subsequent yielding. Progress and pause is extremely important when teaching the rein back

# 7

# Saddling and Mounting

## SADDLING

The most appropriate time to apply the riding saddle for the first time is immediately after the horse has had a driving lesson. He will be settled and perhaps a little tired and thus less likely to perform sudden unwanted movements. The saddle can be fitted after the first driving lesson or any subsequent driving lessons, depending on the general attitude of the pupil. The riding saddle used for the first saddling of the young horse should be reasonably substantial with a girth arrangement that is easy to secure and release and does not call for any undue pushing and pulling of the horse, causing him to be off balance when being fastened. It is often a mistake to apply a light saddle (e.g. 2-5 kg exercise saddle) with which to familiarise the horse—the roller has or should have already achieved the acceptance of the girth application.

The horse must be made to realise he is carrying a substantial and flexible burden when still at this stage of his education. If he is not, perhaps on a windy day when the saddle flaps blow up or the stirrups rattle or touch his ribs, a delayed reaction may eventuate that is quite undesirable.

The horse is held by an assistant in the centre of the yard or sand ring, the driving reins and roller are removed, and the lungeing rein attached to the bit ring or threaded through the bit ring and attached to the head-collar. The saddle cloth is adjusted and the saddle slowly placed in position. The horse is already fully accustomed to the girth and placement of saddle cloths on his back (i.e. the roller) so very little, if any, opposition is encountered in this operation. The stirrup irons should be removed, folded across the saddle, or run up the leathers and secured so that they will not provoke or frighten the horse during the initial saddling and lungeing with saddle.

With the girth fastened securely the horse is led around the perimeter of the enclosure and then lunged at the walk, trot, and canter, both on the off and the near side. When he has accepted the saddle the horse is brought to the centre of the enclosure and the stirrup irons run down the leathers and allowed to dangle, and again he is commanded to walk, trot, and canter. It is essential that the young horse becomes accustomed to the movement of the stirrup irons while he is in motion.

This saddling procedure is carried out after the horse has had a driving lesson and after all his subsequent driving lessons. While the horse is being given a pause in the centre of the enclosure between lungeing exercises the trainer should make a practice of touching and rubbing the saddle and stirrup irons—all the while insisting on the horse standing still and accepting this procedure on both sides.

## MOUNTING

The young horse has been familiarised with bits, reins, rollers, saddles, etc., now he has to become accustomed to a person on his back. This is sometimes accomplished by slowly easing oneself on to the horse bareback, while he is in the confines of a horse box, and gradually riding him around the box. However, this does not always leave a lasting impression for, when the young horse has to leave the box and is presented with an open space and a rider he does not want, the only real lasting impression is the imprint of the would-be rider where he hits the ground.

The opposite is also common practice: that is to apply the saddle, then the rider, and expect the horse to accept both without question. The horse, particularly if he is a proud thoroughbred, can react most indignantly and proceed to show his disapproval in a very violent manner.

Like the sign on the riding school gate:

### WE PLEASE EVERYBODY.

For experienced Riders, we have experienced Horses.

For quiet Riders, we have quiet Horses.

For people who do not like to ride, we have horses that do not like to be ridden.

It is a far better and far safer practice to familiarise a young horse with a rider in the following manner: taking it one stage further from the driving lesson the saddle is fitted, the horse is lunged as previously described, and is then brought to the centre of the enclosure. An assistant again holds the horse's head, insisting on the horse standing still. The person mounting the horse places his foot in the near-side stirrup iron, toe only, colour photo 26, and proceeds to raise and lower himself on the one stirrup iron, familiarising the horse with the extra weight on one side. The girths should be reasonably tight for this procedure so that the saddle will not slip to one side. No riding reins are needed as the assistant is holding the horse with the lungeing rein attached,

and should the horse take exception or move off the person mounting simply steps off and clear of him.

This procedure is then repeated until the rider can mount and place one knee on the saddle as in colour photo 27, with the horse being rubbed on the off side with the hand to familiarise him with a part of the rider being on either side of his body. Remember that a horse's eyes are on the side of his head, and he can see almost as well behind him as he can to his side or to his front.

The rider can now fully mount, slowly at first, but with more movement and fluidity as the horse accepts the procedure. Care must be taken that the stirrup irons are adjusted to enable the rider to mount without overstretching and to ensure that the common habit of the toe protruding into the horse's ribs as the rider mounts does not occur.

Once this initial mounting lesson has been accomplished it should be repeated after each driving lesson until it is accepted as general routine. Mount and dismount on the near side, mount on the near and dismount on the off side. If possible mount on the off side and reverse the procedure, although the mounting on the off side is not easy unless practised, but at least dismount on the off side, insisting all the while and at every mounting lesson that the pupil stands still.

Mounting and dismounting will help prepare the horse mentally as well as physically to accept a rider. If a horse is encountered that refuses to allow a person to mount, in spite of the efforts of an assistant holding the horse's head, then it is best if the horse is tied up so that the rider can mount and dismount until the horse is fully accustomed to the procedure.

There are other methods of making the horse stand still to be mounted, including the use of the nose twitch, hobbling the front legs, or strapping up one foreleg, but the tie-up procedure is commonly the surest and safest method of restraining the horse that is extremely opposed to a person mounting him.

It is ordinary good manners for a horse to stand still while he is being mounted. These are his first lessons at doing this and he will not forget them if they are carried out as previously described.

The saddling and mounting lessons are carried out combined with the driving until the pupil is fully controllable and accepts both the saddle and the person in it as a matter of course.

'When it is considered that the horse has absorbed all this tuition, and his willingness to accept aids, signals, gear, etc., is satisfactory—and he is obviously ready to ride— repeat the driving, saddling, and mouthing procedures for another couple of lessons to be certain of the response.

## RIDING FOR THE FIRST TIME

The pupil now is ready to be ridden off the mark. The day he is ridden for the first time

the whole procedure is carried out thoroughly—driving, saddling, mounting, all in the enclosed yard.

A piece of equipment can be introduced that is a tremendous aid on some horses in this initial riding stage, particularly thoroughbreds, or nervous horses, or highly-strung animals, or when the rider is not confident of retaining control should the horse take exception to being ridden. It is a set of blinkers (see photo 55).

After the horse has been driven and the rider has mounted and dismounted as in the usual lesson, the blinkers are fitted over his bridle and the horse (complete with saddle, etc.) lunged on the off side and then the near side to become used to the restricted vision. This usually does not take more than half a dozen circuits each way to achieve. The youngster is then brought to the centre of the

55. Blinkers of a type used on racehorses

enclosure. Riding reins are fitted in the usual manner, girths checked, and the rider mounts.

The lungeing rein is best dispensed with at this stage: if the horse's education has followed the above procedures there is no need for it in the enclosed area, and it could become a hazard and tangled around the rider if the horse should change direction.

The assistant leads the horse away from the centre of the lungeing area to the outer perimeter, as with the initial lungeing and driving, etc. This time, just grasping the side of the bridle, he leads the horse around a couple of times. While the horse is being led in these circuits of the yard the rider talks to the horse and moves about in the saddle, moving his feet in the stirrup irons and generally letting the horse know that he is on his back. Remember that the blinkers are blocking the horse's rear view.

Having led the horse in a couple of circuits of the yard, the assistant brings the horse to a halt. After a pause the leading continues. The rider then starts to take control, through the reins by feeling the horse's mouth with a slight on and off pressure on the reins. Again the horse is brought to a halt, but this time, although the assistant is still in the leading position, the halt is effected by the rider applying pressure on the mouth via the reins, accompanied by the command to halt—a pause, then continue.

The assistant gradually releases his hold on the bridle, but continues to walk alongside the horse while the rider takes over control via the reins, occasionally effecting a halt, then urging forward movement by leg pressure and the command, taught previously to walk.

When the rider assures the assistant that he feels that the horse is within his control the assistant walks forward and away into the centre of the enclosure, while the rider exercises his control by walking, then trotting, the horse around the enclosure.

With some horses it is best to get them trotting fairly quickly, as they are very slow or tentative at the walk and forward movement under control now is the order of the day.

The use of blinkers for the initial ride is not essential and need only be used when the trainer believes the circumstances warrant them. If not deemed necessary the initial riding procedure is carried out as described, but without the use of blinkers.

The application of the blinkers will be found to have an extremely beneficial effect in focusing the attention and concentration of the young horse, in order to accept the rider's aids and control from the mounted position.

## USE OF BLINKERS

Like young children the ability of young horses to concentrate on a given task for a given period varies tremendously: some may be able to concentrate and accept lessons for twenty minutes or more, others find it difficult to concentrate for five minutes.

For the initial riding procedure it is imperative that the young horse carries out the tasks set for him to the best of his ability, and with as few as possible distractions that tempt or force him into error. The application of blinkers is advantageous in aiding this concentration.

The use of blinkers is not new; they can be traced back to the fourteenth century B.C. They have been used on draught animals for centuries to keep the animal's mind primarily on the task in hand, which is virtually obedience to the aids given without distractions from the wayside or questioning of loads hauled or carried. The use of blinkers for the first ride achieves the same purpose, the obedience to aids without distraction, and thus the establishment of the correct behaviour patterns.

The pupil is now walked, trotted, and slow cantered around the enclosure, turned, and the paces repeated the opposite way, as with the driving. Most horses accept this procedure kindly and willingly; this being the case and the rider having confidence in his ability and the educational standard of his mount, the blinkers if used can be removed after three or four minutes of riding.

The thing for the rider to do now is to dismount and remove the blinkers, and then remount and repeat the riding procedure with the assistant. It is rarely that a horse will buck with a rider when this procedure is carried out thoroughly. Should the young horse have proved extremely nervous or unruly during his previous lessons, or with a horse tending to lean on the bit excessively, the blinkers can be used for a further two or three riding lessons until the rider is satisfied that the pupil is settled and under full control. Should the use of blinkers be deemed not necessary, initial riding is as described, without the blinkers.

The driving is now discontinued and the youngster is saddled daily under normal working conditions and ridden around the enclosure. It may be necessary to lunge the horse for a couple of rounds before riding, as this will settle the horse and allow the girths to be checked for correct tension before mounting. As with the bridle the saddle must be made as comfortable as possible for the horse to bear—no folds of skin doubled under the girths or excess mane jammed under the saddle at the wither.

When the young horse responds satisfactorily within the confines of the enclosure he can then progress to work in a larger or different area, for instance riding through a set of yards or laneways around the farm, etc. Another horse can be an advantage as a companion and as an aid to self-confidence to a shy or nervous youngster, but it is not essential for the average horse that has had the aforementioned education, and with a capable and confident rider in the saddle.

Although it is regarded as safest to initially apply gear, i.e. rollers, saddles, etc., to the young horse when in the safety of the sand ring or similar yard, it is advisable as soon as the pupil accepts these items almost without question to apply them in the box or stables under normal working conditions.

# 8

# Riding

## EXERCISE UNDER A RIDER'S CONTROL

The ability of young horses to accept and manoeuvre with the added weight of a rider varies greatly. In most instances he relies to a large extent on the balance and weight distribution of the rider, this is why it is in the best interests of the horse to have an experienced rider whose sense of balance is *with* the inexperienced horse and not in conflict. Perhaps one of the best exercises that can be practised with the young horse is the figure of eight — the weight of the rider can then be used to advantage in helping the horse to turn and adjust to the change of leg.

An exercise that is often overlooked and not practised enough is riding the horse in a straight line: an object in the distance is lined up with a closer object and the horse ridden (at a trot at first) in a straight line towards the two. To obtain this straight line the horse must be fully under control and the horse and rider completely balanced.

The riding of the young horse for this initial stage should be achieved in a substantial saddle that the rider finds suitable for the occasion. This allows the rider to balance himself without any undue pressure or jerking of the young horse's mouth which, in turn, leads to an all too common fault, that of reining the youngster in in order that the rider should maintain his balance by purchase on the reins, while at the same time urging the horse with voice and/or leg aids to go forward. This type of riding is to be deplored as it leads to all sorts of diabolical problems which are usually blamed on the horse. Remember that the reins on a young horse are the controls and not the safety belt.

The degree of thickness and pliability of riding and lungeing reins, with regard to the feel that can be maintained through them when they are connected with the snaffle bit, has been the subject of some very interesting experiments.

These experiments involved many different riders and young horses and resulted in the conclusions that the slightly stiffer, less-pliable reins — particularly the riding reins — were more suitable once the newness had worn off. They then afforded a more constant contact with the snaffle bit and made it possible to allow the horse a 'loose rein', at times without losing feel or contact with the mouth, whereas the thinner, more-pliable rein tended to sag and lose feel far too easily.

A very effective method of commencing forward movement at a walk from a previously executed halt is: at the same time as the calves of the rider's legs apply pressure to the sides of the horse just behind the girth in the usual aid for the forward movement the verbal aid previously taught, such as 'walk', 'walk on', etc.,

Teaching young horses to swim for exercise is helped by them following an older, experienced horse—not as a coacher but as an example of what to do

is given, accompanied by a push with the knuckles of the hands on the crest of the horse's neck a few centimetres above his wither (see photo 56).

This pushing action will transfer a great deal of the rider's weight on to the forehand of the horse, thus encouraging him to move a step forward to balance the weight. Immediately a response is evident the pushing motion must cease and the conventional leg and/or verbal aids take over.

The pushing must not be overdone, or continued after the horse has learnt to walk forward on command, but for the first few times of proceeding forward calmly from a halt it can

17.   A version of a 'tail rope' that can be used on horses of any age as an aid to promoting forward movement, provided that the horse does not respond by kicking violently

18.   Clean all perspiration stains and marks from the horse after the removal of harness or saddle. If they are not removed the sweat stains and accumulated dirt and grime will cause skin irritations, galls, and scalds, resulting in resentment of harness the next time it is applied.
   Cleaning can range from rubbing with a cloth or brush to a complete hose down as pictured.
   To accustom a young horse to being washed by water from a hose, first familiarise him by leading him into the area in which the washing takes place and standing him for a short period without washing. Before initial hosing wet the horse, particularly the shoulder area, with a damp cloth. Then direct a slow stream of water from the hose on to the dampened shoulder area. This procedure will eliminate most of the apprehension that young horses often display when first they are hosed down

19.   Long reining, or driving, in this manner, is actually an extension of the lungeing procedure

20.   This is a good method of teaching the lungeing exercise, particularly if the initial lessons are carried out in open space with no guiding fences. A training cavesson is fitted to the horse's head and a lunge rein attached to the ring on the top of the noseband or the side of the noseband, whichever is preferred. A bridle is fitted over the cavesson to which is attached a second lunge rein. The trainers position themselves as shown

21.   The first trainer uses the lunge rein from the cavesson as the bearing rein or main control. The second trainer encourages the horse to proceed forward in a circle by moving towards the horse's rear, using his lunge rein from the bit as an additional, though passive, guide

22.   Fitting the roller, or continuous girth

23.   Insist on the horse standing still, but allow him to lunge when the roller is secure

24.   The side rein on the opposite side to the tightened rein should have very little tension, in fact be almost slack, so as not to confuse the horse as to the pressure to which he is supposed to yield.
   Left for short periods in a yard with the gear adjusted in this manner the horse will graduate to yielding to the pressure on the tightened rein, virtually teaching himself to turn in the required direction

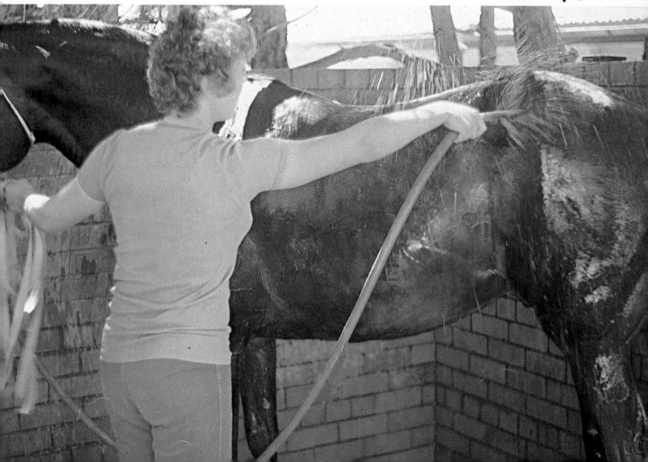

▲17    ▼18

▲19　▼20

▲21 ▼22

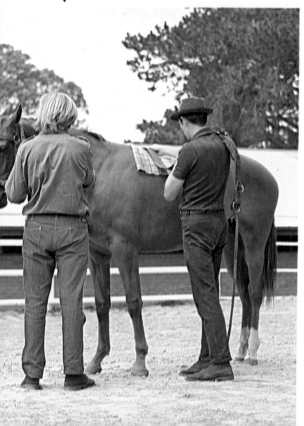

▼23

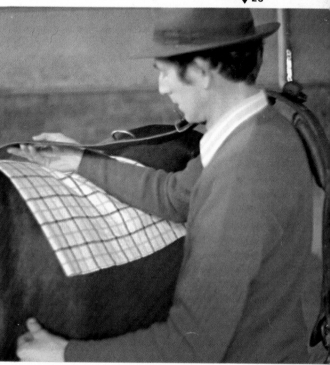

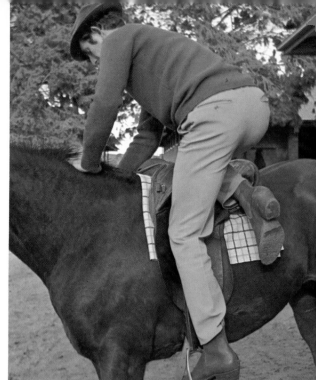

▲26

▲27 ▼28

▲29    ▼30

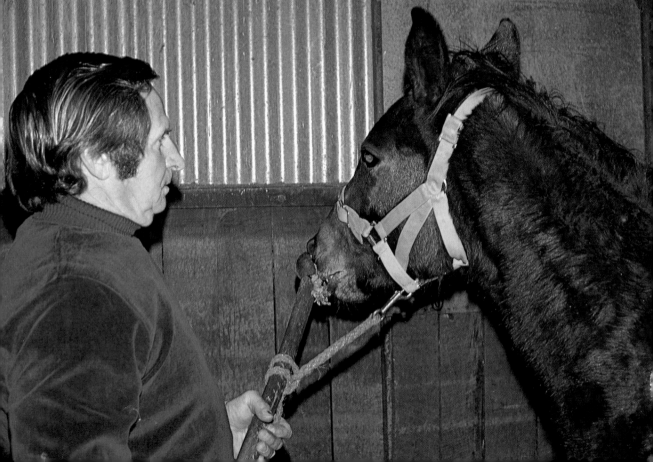

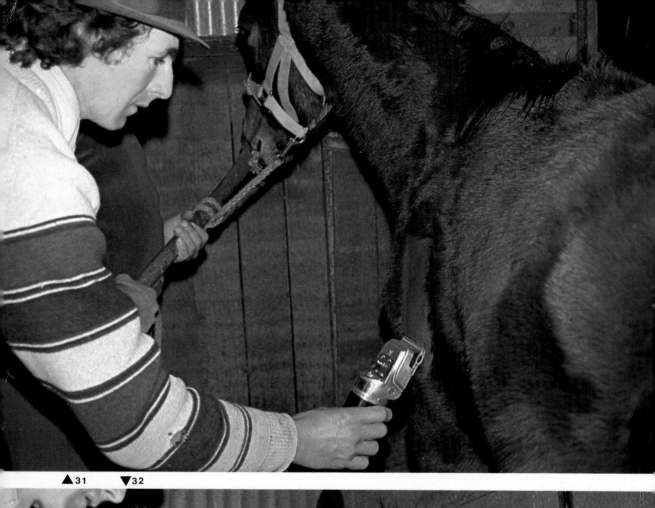

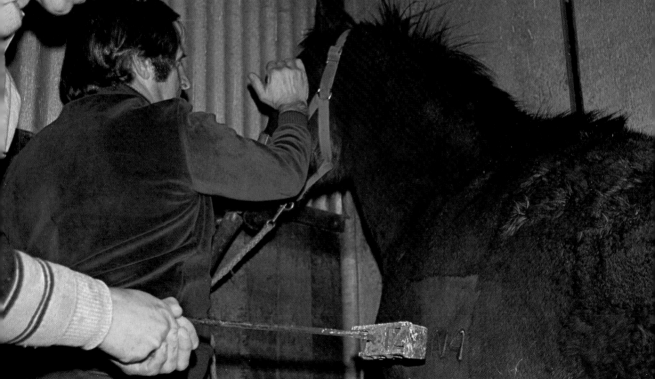

▲31    ▼32

*Captions for colour photos:*

25. To fit the bridle on a horse that takes violent exception to handling around the ears and poll area use the nose twitch as a start to the acceptance of being handled in this area

26. When mounting for the first time the stirrup leather can be lengthened to facilitate easier mounting

27. The toe must be kept well clear of the horse's forearm and girth area. The horse naturally yields to any pressure or discomfort the toe causes if it should touch the horse as the rider mounts. This results in the horse virtually being taught to move away when being mounted which is totally undesirable and often results in the horse being punished for a reaction he was induced to do.

Another undesirable happening involving the same principal as above is the tension on the riding reins being changed as the rider mounts. The reins may have been adjusted to suit the preliminary mounting position (as in colour photo 26) but as the rider springs up and into the saddle the position of the rein hand can change and cause unwanted pressure or jerking of the horse's mouth. This causes the horse to expect a jerk of his mouth as a rider mounts, which results in a similar situation as the toe in the side.

An assistant holding the horse at the head with lead rein attached allows the riding reins to be dispensed with or at least held loosely during the initial mounting lessons

28. With the left hand firmly grasping the mane and the right knee resting on the saddle the trainer can familiarise the animal to the sight and feel of this person being simultaneously on both sides of the horse

29. Two thoroughbred racehorses being trained to gallop fast, while under the control of professional women riders. Although not allowed full extension of pace, the horses are travelling kindly with each rider's style suiting her particular horse's head carriage. Note that the running martingale has come into operation as an aid in preventing the bit from sliding up in the mouth of the horse next to the rails

30. Use of the nose twitch as an aid to restraining a horse and diverting his attention—in this case for fire branding. The cord loop is placed over the upper lip and the handle is twisted until enough pressure is applied to the loop to enable it to stay in position. If excess pressure is applied, or the method abused, violent reaction by the horse can be expected.

The handler stands to one side, not in front of the horse. In this photograph two half hitches of the lead rein have been passed around the twitch handle

31. In preparation for branding, clip off excess hair in the area in which the brand is to be applied. When using electric clippers, accustom the horse to the noise of the motor before attempting to clip.

Immediately prior to applying the clippers to the skin, rub it vigorously with the hand to gain acceptance from the horse to irritation in the area.

The horse's head and neck are inclined towards the side of the operator

32. The horse's vision of the operator is restricted by placing a hand between his eye and the area to be branded, thus lessening the chance of flinching and smudging. As with the initial application of the clippers, the area to be branded should be rubbed by the hand immediately prior to the application of the brand

be used to advantage and eliminate a flailing of the animal's sides with the rider's heels.

## OPEN REIN

The open-rein technique is the easiest rein effect for a young horse to respond to when asked to turn, whether it be from a halt or from a moving gait. The hand controlling the rein on which side the turn is to be effected is carried out to the side and slightly to the front as in photo 57, not pulling to the rear but guiding the horse's head in a kindly manner toward the direction in which he is to travel. This action transfers a great amount of the horse's weight into the same direction, causing him to want to move in that direction in order to maintain a comfortable balance.

Provided that equal pressure of leg aids is maintained and/or the verbal aid for forward movement is used in keeping the horse moving at an even gait, a gentle, even turn is encouraged. If a sharper turn should be required the rider's leg on the turning side is used with more pressure and farther to the rear (see photo 58). The rider's opposite leg can encourage continual forward movement by an on-and-off vibration pressure—the rider easing his weight toward the turn will also assist the horse to grasp what is required of him.

The rein hand on the opposite side of the turn is held below the level of the wither in order to limit the amount of bending if the

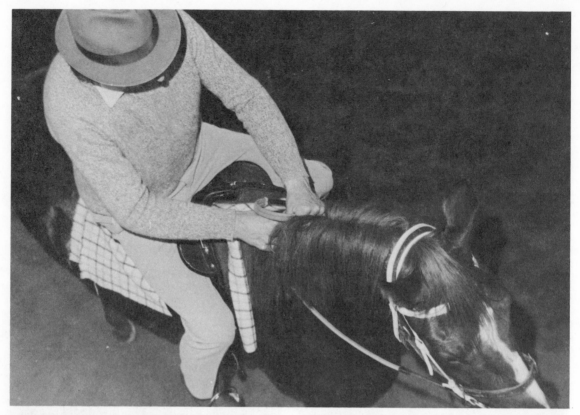

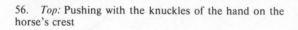

56. *Top:* Pushing with the knuckles of the hand on the horse's crest

57. *Above:* The open-rein technique when asking the horse to turn

58. *Right:* When a sharper turn is required

horse should bend too far into the direction guided. It must be remembered at all times during the basic education of a horse that when a turn or bend is effected in one direction a yielding of the opposite rein must be made available, otherwise the horse may be confused by simultaneous countermanding effects of rein pressures. More advanced rein effects should wait until the horse has thoroughly grasped the basic fundamental principles of forward movement under control, turn, halt, and reverse. Always remember that the ultimate aim is response to almost imperceptible aids.

## DIRECT REIN

The hand controlling the rein on which the turn is to be effected is held slightly to that side and drawn to the rear, to a point where it becomes effective. The hand is held firmly but not rigidly and the fingers should be flexed upon the rein, thus guiding the horse's nose to the side required (see photo 59). The action of the direct rein used in this manner also imposes a great amount of pressure toward the rear which can often have the effect of a decrease in the rate of forward movement whereas, in fact, a turn is required without a

59. The direct-rein technique used for turning

change of pace. What is happening is that the horse is becoming confused as to what is required of him—to turn, to decrease pace, or to halt.

The neck bends toward the side under guidance and the weight of the horse's head and neck is then transferred to the shoulder on that side; this weight then impedes the action of the shoulder and leg and encourages the horse to turn to that particular side in order to maintain a comfortable balance.

The opposite hand must be prepared to yield and not resist the action of the rein being used as a guide.

Although most horses will respond very well to the direct-rein effect when on long reins and being driven from the ground, the addition of a rider's weight when mounted changes the response quite considerably.

It is therefore advantageous to use various degrees of the open-rein technique during basic education under a rider's control until the horse is able to distinguish clearly that the limitation of yield in both reins simultaneously means decrease in pace or halt, and the limitation of yield in one rein only means a turn or inclination of the head is required.

The rider of a horse that is fresh from the kindergarten should be of such a standard that staying on the horse is a natural and automatic achievement to control and complete an exercise with the horse being the primary consideration.

Taking into account the condition of the feet and the surfaces to be ridden over, when the young horse has reached the everyday riding stage he may have to be shod, at least on the forefeet, to combat wear and tear. It is often advisable to postpone shoeing the hind feet during basic education until the muscles are conditioned to exercises under control, and the carrying of a rider. Any overreaching or lapses in co-ordination can be aggravated by hind shoes striking the heels of the forefeet or contacting another leg.

The early riding stage for the racehorse should include an occasional visit to the training track to watch other horses working. If it is possible give the horse a canter along the training area with the rider simulating the jockey position, a position which some horses resent at first. A visit to the starting gates, just to walk him through a few times in company with another horse, should all be part of his basic training (provided that the facilities are available). These things are only some of many which should be checked out before the youngster can be considered to be basically educated.

When leaving a confined area of exercise through a gap or gateway the horse should never be ridden parallel to the surrounding fence or wall and then guided at an angle through the opening. If the horse becomes accustomed to this habit he will naturally veer toward that gate, expecting to go through.

If the horse should be exercised at speed past an opening, such as on a racecourse, he is liable to cause a nasty accident by attempting to rush through the gateway.

When leaving the area the horse should be ridden for a considerable distance past the gateway, turned away from the gate side, ridden back to the opening, and ridden squarely through the opening.

The riding of young inexperienced horses compared to the riding of horses already experienced and adapted to control from the mounted position is poles apart. The experienced horse often takes for granted what he has been trained to do and very often anticipates normal exercise procedure. The young horse, particularly during his first lessons under a rider's control, will often question the aids and directions given by the rider, but do not forget that the horse is a living being and surely has a right to at least question, if only occasionally, the instructions and pressures that are forming his life pattern. Questioning by a horse is sometimes done by ceasing forward movement, reversing, not responding to the bit, attempting to turn in an opposite direction to that directed, and generally employing evasive tactics—such as bucking. These tactics must be discouraged immediately, for once a behaviour pattern is firmly established it becomes almost impossible to erase completely.

## BEHAVIOUR PATTERNS

Great care must be taken to ensure that the behaviour patterns absorbed by the horse are the patterns required permanently. If the horse happens to learn that a certain evasive strategy was effective at some stage, even though it may be temporarily overcome by equipment or a strong-willed rider, if an opportunity presents itself in the future the horse will often revert to these tactics. This is especially so if the horse becomes over-excited.

Some time before leaving the confines of the yard used for initial riding it is a sound practice to extend the pace of the horse to a rousing canter, to ensure that the horse will remain responsive to control when a little excited or extended.

It is all very well in theory to insist that the horse must remain calm at all times while under control, but this is not always possible in practice. A calm state of mind of the horse may be changed by the sight of unfamiliar objects or, and quite often, other horses. For instance quite an interesting and sometimes hazardous situation can arise when a young horse is ridden within sight of a paddock containing other horses.

When the horses in the paddock sight the approaching animal they become excited to varying degrees — from a cursory look to galloping around the paddock and attempting to approach the ridden horse. This is when control by the rider and the degree of the horse's response to the controls becomes complex. The ridden horse often attempts to join in and gallop off with the others, or he may become frightened and attempt to gallop off in the opposite direction. He may even become absolutely frantic in his efforts to do something in some way, in relation to the other horses. Social structure may have some degree of influence.

This behaviour can be minimised or accentuated by the rider and his application of the controls. However, what has basically happened is that inadvertently the horse's state of mind has changed from being calm and responsive to that of being excited and preoccupied and less likely to respond. The degree by which the horse responds to his previously taught commands varies immensely, from total lack of response — resulting in the horse taking complete control — to various degrees of control that enable the rider to effect some influence on the horse.

During a considerable number of experiments involving different horses and riders it was necessary to virtually *educate* the horse to respond to controls while he was in an excited state (not to be confused with the rider initially being the cause of the excited state).

The rider had to *prove* to the horse that he (the rider) was in control and that the control could be maintained. It was noticed that if the rider lost control even for a short space of time, and the horse was aware of the fact, when the manoeuvre was repeated the horse would invariably try to regain control at the same place. The 'association of ideas' capability of the horse was almost unerring in picking the same spot. This association of ideas has a great bearing upon the use of a seasoned racehorse for purposes other than racing.

It is often said that a seasoned racehorse, in order to be used for other purposes (hacking, show work, etc.), has to be re-educated, but this is not entirely so. It is not so much a matter of re-education as a programme of instilling new patterns or extending the behaviour and work patterns of the horse into other fields: a change of abode, a change of diet, a change of saddlery and handlers, a change of work pattern, and most importantly a change of bit.

All these changes coinciding will cause the horse to be aware of new and unfamiliar objects and patterns, causing him to question these procedures. This questioning period can then be used to instil other patterns of behaviour.

The bit is an extremely important change: it does not necessarily have to be a more severe bit than a racing snaffle, nor does it necessarily have to be a milder bit. The main point is that it has to be different in order to make the horse aware of the change.

During a considerable number of trials involving different bits in relation to the change of purpose of racehorses, the half moon three-in-one pelham was proven extremely successful when used with care and combined with the changes mentioned previously.

The seat of the rider is also most important, but the rider should not simulate a jockey's posture in the saddle. All locations resembling a racecourse or training track are best avoided until the new behaviour patterns have been accepted by the horse and response is assured.

There are many other factors also involved, including behaviour patterns established before racing, temperament, etc.

Riding the young horse calls for a very positive approach, not to be confused with abusive approaches which so often seem to be the case. Positive in that the aids and intentions are clear and precise and given in a manner that discourages any doubts the horse has in the rider's ability to control and direct him.

To ensure the best possible control and safety it is a sound policy to test the response to controls while the horse is enthusiastic in his work, within the confines of a yard.

The seat of the rider in the saddle should be balanced in such a manner that his feet in the stirrup irons are slightly forward of the usual hacking position, with the shoulders tending to be square, not leaning forward. If the reverse is practised and the feet are behind the line of the rider's body, plus the shoulders leaning forward, the rider is susceptible to a forward tumble should the youngster prop or falter in mid stride at any pace, be it walk, trot, or canter.

When giving the young racehorse his first lessons on the training area, with the rider simulating a jockey's posture, it is best to ride with the reins forming a short bridge, which is rested just forward of the horse's wither. This manner of riding will greatly assist collection and will help prevent a forward tumble should

the horse prop or drastically reduce his forward momentum.

## THE RIDING WHIP

Although the reins are best controlled individually, to give greater scope for guidance and perhaps to emphasise a particular manoeuvre, the use of a single bridge (one handed) is often necessary if the rider chooses

*Project* the voice to the horse when giving or teaching commands.

to use a whip. The use of a riding whip is optional but in many cases not entirely necessary as reins and leg aids, coupled with the rider's voice—often reassuring, sometimes coaxing, occasionally harsh and demanding (but never shouting)—will usually produce a responsive youngster.

However, it is hardly fair on the young horse if his basic education does not include familiarisation with a rider carrying a whip when later, as in the case of the racehorse, a rider is legged up, whip in hand, and the horse is given a smart slap to remind him to jump out of the starting gates, or for numerous other reasons.

Perhaps it is in the best interests of the horse for the rider to at least carry a riding whip and acquaint him with it by rubbing it lightly on the sides of the neck, and to carry it in both the right and the left hands. In the case of a reluctant horse the whip is a distinct advantage, as a smart tap over the quarters will save a lot of conflict of ideas between horse and rider and encourage a tardy animal to proceed with forward movement.

If the riding whip is to be used, remember to use it over the horse's hindquarters, well behind his hip; do not hit a horse in the flank or the stifle joint as this will tend to make him sour and shorten stride instead of lengthening it. The use of a whip down a young horse's shoulders is questionable as it rarely does any good, more often it causes a resentment and retaliation in the form of a pig root, bucking, or rearing.

The use of the whip on the forequarters of a young horse should be restricted to scrubbing along the neck in combination with the reins. The carrying of a whip can be done by most riders, but the use of a riding whip to its best advantage—as an aid—should be left to the rider practised in such an art.

## RIDING IN COMPANY

Often encountered in riding young horses, particularly when a number of horses are being educated at the same time, is their reluctance to go 'upsides'—alongside or in between other horses with riders. There are perhaps a number of reasons that have to be considered before attempting to overcome this reluctance. The most common factor which deters a youngster from going upsides willingly appears to be the rider on the *other* horse, especially if that rider is moving about in the saddle and attempting to coax his own mount closer to the horse in question.

Another thing that is often overlooked is the fact that some horses seem to exude a dominating influence, which appears to deter a weaker-willed horse from close association, quite apart from the usual deterrent of kicking which is always a risk when a number of horses are in close proximity to one another. Yet again, a weaker-willed horse may resent being placed in a position where he is susceptible to buffeting or squeezing by other horses and riders.

A successful method of overcoming the reluctance of a young horse to proceed with forward movement in close proximity with other horses and riders is to take two horses into a sand ring or small yard—12 to 13 m in diameter is ideal—and ride them at a trot in circling work, the horses being positioned on opposite sides of the enclosure. After they are accustomed to this circling work in company, one horse is ridden to the centre of the enclosure and made to stand while the other horse continues the circling work around him. When the horse in the centre has accepted the movements of his companion around him the positions are reversed, with the circling horse being brought to the centre.

As the horses become accustomed to this procedure the horse requiring the education is worked at a trot around the perimeter of the enclosure. The other horse is worked in small circles around the centre of the enclosure, but with these circles gradually widening so that the centre horse will be approaching the outside horse. In an area such as a 12 to 13 m ring the centre horse will be walking at first, until an increase of pace is necessary as his circles widen.

The centre horse should always be kept a little behind the line of progress of the outside horse, otherwise the outside horse will prop and tend to stop or turn back—the enclosing fence or wall will prevent him from escaping from the advance of the inside horse. Although the trot is often best for the purpose, the gait for the initial exercises of this nature (as soon as the horses show a semblance of accepting one another) can be reduced to a walk and changes of direction in pairs can be practised. Any number of horses can be added to the line in this fashion, depending on the size of the enclosure.

The riding of colts and fillies in close proximity to each other often creates problems such as the colts becoming precocious and difficult to control, often the cause of rearing, and the fillies may come in season, become sluggish, and more interested in other horses rather than the task in hand.

To perform well in the field required of him the horse must be educated to adapt to the conditions under which he is to perform. Acquainting him with these conditions at this basic educational period gives him a distinct advantage, and also gives owners, trainers, and riders an idea as to how his temperament is going to affect his future performance. It is essential that the horse learn to respond to controls and to obey his rider only, not reacting to other horses and activities which may be going on around him. Provided that he is sufficiently advanced in his response to controls to be able to cope with and absorb benefits from these experiences, they can be included in his basic education.

It is beneficial, for instance, for the young potential show horse to visit a show or similar function a few times even though he is not taking a competitive part. He may be a highly-priced future contender for the country's top shows, but an occasional visit to the local gymkhana as a spectator will do him a lot of good.

Similarly, the young racehorse has to learn to adapt to situations such as horses galloping past him while he is only required to proceed at a slower gait. The sooner the young performing horse is acquainted with these situations the better.

When assessing horses performances, it is foolhardy to generalise on the time required to teach a horse to respond to an aid or command, as every horse is an individual: flexibility and commonsense must prevail.

The exercises and lessons are, of course, carried out regularly in an everyday pattern. An exception to this is if a horse reaches a stage in basic education when it does not seem willing to complete that particular lesson and is completely stale and unresponsive. This can occasionally happen with horses of doubtful temperament, horses that have travelled long distances immediately prior to the basic education procedure, or horses in low physical condition.

A few days of complete rest will work wonderfully well and, when the horse's lessons are resumed, he will be in a more receptive frame of mind and invariably respond far more willingly to the tasks asked of him. It is not always possible to trace and identify a reason why the horse is not responding to a particular aid or lesson, e.g. damage to interior of mouth,

pain caused by teething, abcess forming in ears or other places, possible bruising to girth area, etc. The rest period over a few days will give any minor problem a chance to heal, or any potentially major problem time to become obvious. It will also give the thinking horseman time to evaluate the cause of the problem.

On the other hand, another type of horse may need a good smart slap or two with the lunge whip or riding whip. It is the trainer who must evaluate each particular situation, and think before applying any severe chastisement.

The retention of a memory pattern by the horse is mainly by repetition and an association of ideas, for example the same aid is given for the same manoeuvre in the same place. But it is also a fact that a horse will react to the application of pain. A hypodermic needle need only be used once on the horse for him to retain a distinctly unpleasant memory of it. The same applies to the use of a whip or a severe bit.

Each individual has a certain level of tolerance to the acceptance of pain on different parts of the body and when these levels are reached the acceptance of pain ceases to be repressed and retaliation takes place. When a horse is subjected to severe pain he will often revert to his natural instinct of flight and/or defence.

A young horse undergoing basic education should never be subjected to demands for perfection in any manoeuvre or response. First the horse has to be educated to respond to aids or signals after which he has to learn to respond to these signals in a safe and practical manner. The way to perfection is to gain success to a satisfying degree on a rising scale.

To produce a willing, safe, and well-mannered animal, ready for further schooling in his particular field of work, the trainer can adapt the methods described or vary them to suit the needs of the individual horse.

# 9
# Overcoming Problems

## THE HABITUAL REARER

This is quite a problem, and a dangerous one, for which various solutions have been tried. These solutions range from bursting a container of water between the horse's ears while he is actually rearing to jumping off the horse and pulling him over backwards. Most of them require a degree of gymnastic skill for questionable results.

The majority of horses that rear habitually are using this undesirable practice as an excuse to escape from, or to evade proceeding with, forward movement. This evasion of forward movement can be caused by a number of reasons and each horse's reason must be found in the early stages in order to rectify the situation.

In some instances the horse can be very quick to realise that when he rears the rider is placed at a distinct disadvantage and loses control of the horse. However, the horse gains control of the rider and, if the horse's nature is such that he will seek to make capital of this, he will continue to rear and gain more control over the rider—even though the cause of the original rearing has been rectified.

One of the most common, and most difficult, of horses that rear is the one that rears, whips around while he is in the air, and lands facing in the opposite direction. There follows a method of curing this habit which has

proved to be extremely effective and which incorporates the maximum of safety to the rider.

The requirements are an anti-rearing bit, a headstrap, an extra set of reins, a running martingale, and a positive and experienced rider. The rearing bit is fitted as an addition to the usual snaffle bit, etc. It has a separate headstrap and is left slightly loose in the mouth. Very often the horse has a particular place where he begins his rearing. If this is the case he can be saddled and bridled as usual, plus the addition of the anti-rearing bit with the lead rein attached and led, first without and then with the rider, past the spot.

If and when he rears, a tug on the anti-rearing bit—see photo 60—will bring the horse back to earth smartly. Care must be taken not to abuse the animal with this bit as it is quite severe, but if used with care and common-sense it is very effective. The idea is to convince the horse that it will hurt him to do this thing, therefore the bit must only come into operation when the horse is in the air.

The moment of application of pain or severe discomfort to the horse must be accompanied by a signal—such as a harsh, demanding tone of voice—in order to convince the horse he is doing wrong. Once this signal has been established in conjunction with the use of the anti-rearing bit by the assistant the lead rein can be dispensed with and the extra set of reins,

attached to the single ring on the anti-rearing bit, passed through a running martingale which is adjusted reasonably short and thence to the rider, who can use the anti-rearing bit as deemed necessary if the horse should attempt to rear. Timing is the essence of success.

## SHYING HORSES

Familiarity is the best cure with most horses that shy from objects that are strange to them. Occasionally a horse will use this apparent shyness as an excuse for not proceeding with forward movement.

Firmness by the rider is the cure with horses that shy away from objects such as white posts, drain holes, and numerous other common articles. It is often the custom to force the horse right up to the object and show him that it will not hurt him and that there is nothing to be feared.

This practice, however, can easily be overdone. If the purpose of the exercise was to make the horse take notice of the object in question, exactly the same principle would apply, so it is perhaps better to consistently ride the horse past the object. He will soon understand that that object is not there specifically to frighten him—or for him to take notice of—but an ordinary, everyday part of the scenery. A staid and true-going horse as a companion is a distinct advantage.

Considerable consideration must be shown toward young horses when they shy away from or are hesitant in approaching objects or situations that resemble instinctive hazards. The horse's natural instinct for survival motivates him to show caution with such things as drain holes in the roadsides, changes in the surface of the terrain, 'unsure of his footing', etc.

Time spent on showing the animal that the going is safe, even to the extent of dismounting and leading the horse over or past the obstacle before remounting and riding him past or over, is time well spent. It is also far safer for horse and rider than forcing or physically abusing the animal to proceed against his in-built survival instincts.

When riding a young horse, or any horse for that matter, read the road ahead for possible trouble spots, anticipate as far as possible what the horse would take exception to and act accordingly.

Blinkers may be used in extreme cases with a racehorse as shying at speed or during a race is an extremely dangerous practice.

61. A method of lessening the severity of an anti-rearing bit by attaching the lead rein to the headcollar ring in addition to the bit ring.

This photograph also shows how a horse can be given cause to rear or be 'touchy' around the head by the corner of the metal used for the junction of the cheek strap, nose band, lower chin strap, and bit attachment digging into the bony protuberance known as the facial crest. This can cause a nasty sore and result in a violent reaction when the horse is touched in this area. The condition occurs frequently when a headcollar is left on a young horse and not adjusted periodically to allow for the growth of the animal *(Photo courtesy News Ltd)*

60. *Facing page:* A violent and high-rearing horse about to receive a tug on the anti-rearing bit while he is in the air. Care must be taken to keep the lead rein away from the forelegs of a horse that 'paddles' or strikes *(Photo courtesy News Ltd)*

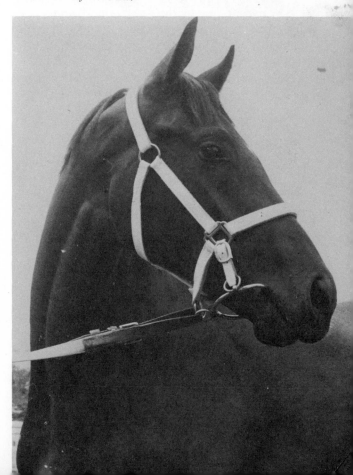

A sheepskin noseband or shadow roll sometimes improves a young horse's concentration on the work in hand if the reluctance to go forward is caused by ground orientated shadows, change of road surface, etc. The noseband or shadow roll obscures these potential hazards from the horse's view and restricts his downward vision.

## NERVOUS HORSES

Nervousness in the young horse in the form of trembling, perspiring, and a generally timid outlook on life, is often associated with hereditary traits passed down through the sire's or dam's breeding, provided that the youngster

Remember—It is the *tone* of the voice that can command a horse's attention.

has not been subjected previously to any violent mistreatment.

Nervous reaction to a situation can range from a tensing of the muscles—accompanied by questioning by the sight, sound, and smell-ing senses—to wide-eyed trembling and perspiring, and to panic; the latter can be accompanied by an attempt at flight. In between these extremes is a condition which could be described as nervous energy. In a horse which has a reasonably tractable nature, but possessing a nervous quality, this often adds a sense of presence and pride to his general being. Thoroughbreds, particularly the strain bred to compete in sprint races, often display this nervous energy.

Repetition and familiarisation is the keynote during the basic education of nervous horses, particularly the place of abode. Placing the horse repeatedly in the same box or yard for his rest periods will give him a chance to unwind and relax in surroundings that are familiar to him. This applies to all horses but especially to horses that are highly strung. The company of a steadier and more settled horse during his work periods is of considerable benefit.

The diet of a horse can have quite a considerable bearing on his reactions to situations: the higher the energy level of the diet the more keyed up the horse can become.

# 10
# Practical Feeding

## HINTS ON THE PRACTICAL FEEDING OF HORSES

*1. The effects of the ration on the horse should be closely observed.*

Scientific calculation alone will not ensure a practical ration. Assess the horse's body size and bone structure when deciding on the optimum stage of condition. The horse that is gaining too much condition on pasture alone can be shifted to less luxurious pasture, or have grazing time restricted by confinement (e.g. stabled overnight), or undergo increased exercise to maintain ideal body weight. If, however, a horse is gaining weight on supplementary feeding or is totally reliant on a prepared ration (i.e. stabled horses) then, to reduce condition to a suitable level, decrease the amount of energy-rich component in the ration (usually the grain), or decrease the total amount of ration being fed, or again increase the amount of exercise the horse receives.

The horse that is losing or not gaining condition on adequate grazing or a reasonable ration may be having too much exercise, or may need to have teeth or feet inspected and be dewormed to ensure that body condition returns to normal. Lactating mares may require extra rations to ensure that they maintain condition for adequate milk supply to the foal and for further breeding.

*2. The ration should be palatable, economical, practical, and supply the horse's requirements.*

Rations need not be complicated mixtures and most can be made from ingredients available locally.

Some horses may not find a ration quite as palatable as other horses, so that often the addition of a small amount of molasses (up to five per cent of the total ration) will make it more attractive. However, don't use molasses or other sweet, palatable substances to cover up poor-quality ingredients, especially high-fibrous roughage.

A high-quality ration will supply all the requirements including vitamins and minerals for horses at rest, or those performing normal work, without the addition of expensive supplements. However, horses undergoing long and strenuous work loads, including heavy lactation, or suffering from certain mineral or vitamin deficiencies, may benefit from such a supplement.

*3. The ration must be balanced between ingredients of roughage (hay chaff, pasture) and concentrates (oats, bran, protein meals, etc.).*

Roughage alone, while supplying the needs of the horse at rest or performing light or occasional work, does not allow for the efficient performance of continuous or heavy work. However, too much concentrate, while providing energy for work, can lead to digestive upsets (e.g. colics, founder, etc.). Thus an optimum balance varies from total pasture feeding where roughage is the sole nutrient source, to a fifty per cent roughage—fifty per cent concentrate ration, depending on such factors as the work load, age, stage of growth, pregnancy or lactation, or performance requirements.

### 4. Avoid sudden changes in ration proportions or ingredients.

Sudden changes of this type can lead to digestive upsets or loss of appetite. A slow replacement over seven to ten days or longer is necessary for changes such as from old to new season's hay or grain. Ideally three to four weeks is best for radical ingredient changes, e.g. from oats to barley or pellets. Some horses are particularly sensitive or allergic to certain feeds, and a sudden change may cause severe digestive or skin disorders, or may lead to such conditions as founder.

If a horse is brought in from pasture to be stabled and fed entirely on prepared rations, it is best to add only about five or ten per cent of the planned grain level initially and gradually increase the amount to the required level over a period of one to two weeks. This increase should also match the increase in the level of work or exercise. Any sudden increases in the amount of work or exercise should be avoided because they may cause muscle stiffness or soreness: these increases should also be spread out over a similar period of one to two weeks, corresponding to the grain or ration increase.

### 5. Restrict grain intake on days when the horse is resting.

The horse may suffer digestive upsets, or conditions such as founder, if allowed to consume a large proportion of grain in the ration without work or exercise. This is important to remember on those days when the horse is not worked, for, besides causing digestive problems or becoming difficult to handle due to the high energy content of the ration, the sudden increase in exercise when the horse is again

worked may lead to such conditions as azoturia. This condition should not occur if the grain content is reduced to about one-third of the normal amount on days when the horse is not exercised. The moderate decrease in the grain content should not cause any adverse reactions.

### 6. Modify rations to suit particular horses.

Horses differ in appetite, and likes or dislikes, so modify the rations to suit the individual horse in order to obtain the best results. Horses with continually poor appetites may need a ration which contains a larger proportion of concentrate and less roughage to keep them interested in their feed and to enable them to derive sufficient nutrients to perform at the same level as other horses. They may find some foods unpalatable and may require the addition of sweetening substances such as molasses. To avoid the selection of particular ingredients make sure that the rations are well mixed. Some horses require more food than others although they are performing the same work, others are allergic to certain foodstuffs—usually shown by skin bumps, colics, etc.—so change ingredients if necessary.

### 7. Avoid feeding dusty, mouldy, or contaminated ingredients.

Dusty foods can cause respiratory problems—to reduce the amount of dust either damp down the ration with warm water or warm liquid molasses, or sieve the grain before mixing the ration. Mouldy hay or grains may contain poisons which can produce digestive upsets such as diarrhoea or colics, or the loss of unborn foals. Feeds contaminated by weevils, rat or mice dung, etc., can cause various diseases in horses. Feed infected with poisonous seeds or plants may cause poisoning in horses ingesting it. Feed infected with weeds or weed seeds can cause a build up of weeds in a grazing area, because they may be spread during wastage of the feed or they may pass through the horse undigested. Ideally weeds should be kept to a minimum in grazing paddocks as the increase in fertility levels of the soil around the manure areas will encourage weed growth. Horses are also very selective grazers and this can lead to an increase in unwanted species of weeds. Before a horse is introduced to a new paddock a check should be made for poisonous plants.

*8. Regularly observe the horse's feeding habits.*

A sudden poor appetite could mean bad health or colic, etc. Sudden bursts of hard work, besides leading to possible muscle disorders, may sometimes cause a horse to lose appetite for a short time. Change in ration ingredients may cause a decrease in appetite if any of the ingredients are unpalatable to the horse. However, if the horse is consistently not consuming all his rations the amount of food may be too great, especially when normal body weight or work effort is being maintained.

Clean out any food that the horse does not eat each day, and do not allow access to food that has been wet in the food bin, or contaminated by manure or foreign matter. If the horse leaves long straws in the feed bin, or small balls of wet, chewed food (called quidding), it is an indication that his teeth may need inspection and rasping, or that his mouth or gums are painful (e.g. teething, grass seeds, etc.).

*9. The ration must be fed regularly — even during holidays.*

The horse is a creature of habit and should be fed at the same times every day, and ideally three to four times a day when stabled and being fed prepared rations. This is because the horse has a small stomach, no gall bladder, and chews its food slowly; therefore an almost continuous but controlled amount of food should be provided to prevent overeating or a sudden high-energy intake. If the horse is pastured and relies on a small supplementary prepared ration, it is usually only necessary to feed this ration once daily. Always try to feed the horse after exercise, after allowing twenty to thirty minutes for him to cool down. However, if

feeding before exercise, then allow two or three hours' interval before work to avoid exercising on a full stomach. Do not work a horse *directly* after feeding as this can lead to digestive upsets, cramps, and colics.

For ponies that are at pasture and not fed a supplementary ration during the week because they receive limited exercise, it is a good idea to feed a small prepared ration on the weekend when the horse is going to be ridden and exercised for longer periods. Feed about half the grain or energy supplement allocated, mixed with about double its weight of a roughage such as chaff, two to three hours before the pony is worked (e.g. taken to a pony club). The remainder can then be fed twenty to thirty minutes after the pony is returned to pasture and has cooled off.

If the horse is stabled or confined to a small yard, and fed a prepared ration, then ideally the ration should be split into three or four portions, feeding one part early in the morning, one part about midday, one part in the evening, followed by a portion of good-quality hay as roughage to chew and digest overnight. If exercise is performed at any set time, e.g. ponies that are usually worked after school, then it is best to include about half the grain component in the feed ration which is fed ideally at least two to three hours before an exercise period. However, this may need to be fed in the morning ration as the midday ration is often not convenient to feed, due to school or job commitments.

*10. The ration should be fed in the same place.*

Locate the feed bin in a sheltered place, preferably under some type of shed or shelter, and leave it there. The horse will know where the feed bin is and usually will be waiting there at regular feed times. Avoid shifting it around a yard or paddock unless it becomes excessively boggy in wet weather, as this can cause erosion in each area where the horse stands to feed: it is better to erode one area only than to spoil many areas of the pasture. Locate the feed bin in a position that is close to the food storage area to prevent carrying the feed too far. Be sure to secure any stored food properly to prevent the pony helping himself and overeating, leading to serious digestive upsets and possible colic or founder.

### 11. Do not feed concentrates on the ground.

Provide an adequate container with no sharp edges, a flat base, and heavy enough to prevent the horse tipping it over and spilling the feed. Concentrated feeds on the ground are quickly scattered, pawed into the ground, and wasted. Fossicking around on the ground for tasty concentrates can increase the parasite burden and, in sandy yards, the horse can ingest large quantities of sand as he searches for food, which can lead to sand colic. Ideally the feed bin should be raised to the height of the horse's chest to decrease contamination with manure.

### 12. Do not allow a horse to eat concentrates too rapidly.

Most horses that eat concentrates (e.g. grain, etc.) quickly become prone to digestive upsets. This can be prevented by carefully mixing the grain with the roughage component, e.g. chaff. A small amount of the grain can be lightly sprinkled on top of this mixture to attract the horse if he is a shy feeder. A salt brick or stone placed in the bottom of the feeder will make the horse search to pick up the concentrate and thus slow down his intake.

### 13. Measure the amount of food by weight rather than volume.

Grains, especially, can change in seed size and weight due to seasonal variations and to ensure that a horse receives the same amount every time the ration ingredients should be

measured by weight rather than volume. Therefore when a new bag is opened, or ingredients are obtained from a different source, weigh the ingredients to check them and then make volume adjustments accordingly. A small spring balance with the measured amount of feed placed in a small plastic bag is ideal to check weight for volume.

14. *Feed hay at night and preferably in small lots.*
As mentioned previously it is best to give hay as the last feed of the day, to prevent the horse being hindered by a distended and full digestive tract. The horse can consume the hay slowly and allow adequate time for digestion. In a group of horses at pasture the hay should be placed in above-ground hay racks, or in piles far enough apart to prevent fighting and spoilage: one more pile than the number of

horses present will reduce any squabbling. Make sure that strings or wire are removed from bales or sheaves, and check for souring and moulds before allowing the horses to eat it. Most horses tend to waste a fair proportion of cereal-type hays and therefore roughage of this type is best chaffed to prevent such waste.

15. *The ration must be well mixed.*
Rations should be carefully mixed to prevent the horse selecting certain ingredients, especially grains, and either leaving the remainder or suffering digestive upsets. Make sure there are no lumps of minerals, especially salt (apart from the salt lick) as this can lead to serious digestive upset. Always mix the feed in small amounts daily and do not store mixed feeds for longer than one day, especially if they are dampened to reduce dust or contain such

Horses need shelter from the elements. Shelter can range from a constructed windbreak to capitalising on trees in their natural condition. This pastoral scene shows how difficult it is to improve on nature

ingredients as liquid molasses or oils. Store the mixed food in a vermin and fly proof container to prevent contamination and spoilage.

16. *Regularly clean food and water containers.*

Food containers should be kept clean to avoid build up of dirt and moulds which can cause digestive upsets. Water troughs should be checked daily and cleaned regularly to prevent the build up of algae and sludge from chewed food. Water buckets should be heavy enough to prevent the horse tipping them over or lifting them around with his teeth, and preferably secured in a frame or to a fence or post.

17. *Check the horse daily for signs of ill-health.*

Check the horse daily to ensure he is eating, drinking, passing manure, and urine. A horse standing alone, rolling frequently, dull, or slow to begin feeding should be checked for colic, founder, or other sickness.

18. *Provide some form of shelter.*

A shelter, or trees, should be available during hot weather, and some type of windbreak in very cold weather. Horses with little shelter during the winter will need extra energy in their ration to maintain body temperature, etc., and will be prone to sickness due to cold stress.

19. *Avoid feeding lawn cuttings.*

On no account should lawn clippings be fed to horses as they can cause digestive upsets and colics. They can also contain residual chemical poisons, leaves of poisonous garden plants such as oleander, and other foreign matter (e.g. glass, metal, stones) that can cause serious complications.

## PONY NUTRITION

Ponies require a balanced ration to provide nutritive compounds for maintaining body functions, condition, and general good health. An adequate ration should be supplied at all times—especially during periods of growth and productive activity, e.g. training, riding, pregnancy, and rearing a foal.

Although horses can thrive on a large variety of foods, generally only a few types are available locally to the horse owner or trainer. Better performance results can be obtained, and health maintained, by careful selection of food ingredients and by obeying certain rules of feeding. While practical feeding of a horse requires careful observation of the horse's condition and performance by the owner or trainer, scientific calculations can give an estimate of the amount, composition, and adequacy of the ration that is being used or is planned. Apart from making sure that the needs of the horse are entirely satisfied, rations should be composed of ingredients that are easily obtainable, economical, uncomplicated, of good quality, and palatable to the horse.

Careful attention to feeding should be complemented by adequate exercise and general health care of the horse, including regular grooming, attention to the feet, teeth, and parasite control in order to get maximum benefit from the ration being fed. Horses differ in their requirements with regard to the proportion and amount of feed ingredients due to factors such as body weight, rate and stage of growth, age, work intensity and duration, reproductive requirements, and their individual food-conversion capabilities. Therefore the ration should be planned with these factors in mind and should supply the horse with an acceptable, balanced diet at the least cost.

**A. Components of the ration**

The ration must contain sources of energy, protein, fibre, minerals, and vitamins, as well as an adequate supply of clean, fresh water. It is important that the need for and use of these essentials is studied when planning a ration.

1. *Energy.*

Energy is required to maintain vital muscle activity, synthesis of various body compounds, and body temperature. A basic amount of energy is required by each horse, which is called the *maintenance energy* requirement, and this is proportional to the body weight of the horse. Extra energy is needed for productive activity such as work, pregnancy, lactation, and maintaining body temperature in cold weather, etc., otherwise the horse will lose weight or decrease productive output. Energy that is not used in maintenance, or work, is stored as fat within the body, so that excessively fat horses are an indication of an oversupply of energy or lack of exercise. In this case the excess fat can be reduced either by increased exercise or by decreasing the energy intake in the food: this must be remembered especially if fat ponies are at pasture during the lush spring growth when pasture has a higher water content, as they can be very prone to founder.

Energy in the diet is primarily supplied by starch and some other soluble carbohydrates (mainly from grains in the ration), cellulose (from pasture, roughage, and the fibrous portion of grains), as well as fat which is present in most types of feed. Excess protein in the diet will also provide some energy, but this is an inefficient and expensive form of energy supply and should be avoided. Grains supply about twice as much energy as roughages, whereas fats supply about twice that of starches (grains), but the horse can only tolerate about ten per cent of fat in the diet.

Energy input has to be adjusted to cover requirements due to work intensity and duration, the effects of the weather, condition of the horse, and the horse's own individual efficiency—as some horses will perform better than others on similar rations. Grain supplementation during periods of growth or work will supply needed extra energy, whereas the horse at rest requires little or no grain depending on the quality and quantity of the pasture or hay (this is especially true for the pony doing only occasional light work or being ridden on weekends or after school). In general, ponies—unless they are working very hard, are pregnant, are rearing a foal, or are turned out during very cold weather—do not need grain in their rations. However, an oversupply of energy-poor roughage or pasture can result in poor stamina, dull coat, and poor working ability. To obtain sufficient nutrients from this fibrous food large quantities are consumed and the pony can develop a distended gut or 'hay belly'. A small amount of grain may need to be added to the ration, but too much may result in a pony becoming more highly spirited and difficult to handle, or can produce severe digestive upsets.

*2. Protein.*
Proteins in the food are broken down during

Keep pasture free from contamination to ensure the healthy growth of horses such as are seen in this photo

digestion into substances called amino acids, and these in turn are used by the body to build vital body proteins, hair, hooves, and muscle. The body requires some essential amino acids which must be obtained from proteins in the food, whereas others are synthesised during the digestive processes. There is a decrease in protein needs inversely proportional to the age of the horse because growth of muscle, etc., is more rapid immediately after foaling and gradually slows down until maturity is reached. Breeding horses also require more dietary protein than maintenance horses. It is often convenient and a cheaper practice to provide a higher protein concentrate ration for young growing horses, breeding and lactating mares, and working stallions, whereas maintenance horses will usually only require protein levels obtained in pasture and hays.

Excess protein can be utilised as an energy supply but it is not economic to oversupply protein, as protein supplements are more expensive than grains or other energy supplements. Proteins are contained in pastures, good roughages, and grain, but higher protein sources are obtainable from vegetable meals such as soya bean meal, linseed meal, and safflower, sunflower, and pea meals or seeds. These are cheaper and generally of better quality and more palatable to the horse than the animal protein meals, such as bone meal, fish meal, and meat meal.

## 3. Fibre.

Fibre which is usually obtained from pasture and roughages, as well as the fibrous covering of some grains (e.g. oats), is important as it helps to keep the digestive mass open which is essential for efficient digestion. The fibre content of roughages varies considerably, increasing as the plants mature.

Older horses can digest fibre more readily than young horses, and it is especially important that a low-fibre ration be fed to foals, as they do not have the specialised gut development necessary for fibre digestion. Therefore they usually grow poorly and develop distended gut or 'hay belly' if fed high-fibre roughages before or soon after weaning. However, large amounts of high-fibre, poor-quality roughage should be avoided in all horses as it can produce a similar effect.

## 4. Minerals.

Although mature horses can perform moderate work for extended periods on rations composed mainly of grass, hay, and some cereal grains, larger amounts of minerals may be required during periods of growth, pregnancy, or lactation.

Dietary requirements for minerals are dependent on the body weight on the horse, the growth rate, amount of work, the loss in sweat, and the availability of each mineral in the diet. Minerals are needed for body development as well as for maintenance and, in addition to providing adequate levels, they should be offered in balanced proportions. This is especially so for calcium, phosphorus, and salt. Calcium and phosphorus, in conjunction with Vitamin D, are important in bone growth, and to ensure freedom from bone disorders the proportion of these minerals in the ration must be carefully controlled.

The young horse requires about one-and-a-half times to twice the amount of calcium to phosphorus to ensure best bone development, whereas the mature horse can tolerate much greater calcium levels, up to four to five times that of phosphorus, without any mineral imbalance. Vitamin D plays an important part in the control of the ratio of calcium to phosphorus, and good-quality food and sunlight, which indirectly supplies Vitamin D by synthesis in the skin, will aid in the utilisation and proper balance of these minerals.

Salt provision is also important—especially for working horses, as they excrete salt in their sweat and a deficiency can lead to nervous disorders, poor working ability, and reduced appetite. Normally a horse at pasture will consume enough salt during grazing, but horses performing moderate or heavy work will need a salt supplement. This is best given as rock salt, table salt, or specialised proprietary animal salt compounds. Salt licks as blocks are sometimes provided, but the amount of salt intake cannot be accurately estimated and can vary according to taste and individual habits.

About sixty grams of salt daily need to be added to the diet of a mature horse under average conditions, and under hot conditions or strenuous exercise up to ninety grams. Ponies require about forty grams and sixty grams respectively.

Most other minerals are usually adequately supplied in good-quality feeds but the provision of a trace-element supplement mixed in the ration is useful in ensuring proper mineral balance, especially in growing horses and pregnant or lactating mares. Minerals of any type, if added to the rations, must be well mixed into the feed to avoid digestive or toxic disturbances.

## 5. Vitamins.

Although vitamin requirements are thought to be generally low in the horse, an adequate supply is essential for good health and maintenance.

A lot of vitamins are synthesised during the processes of digestion which, along with good-quality food ingredients, should supply most of the horse's requirements. Rapidly growing, pregnant, lactating, or heavily worked horses may require extra vitamin supplementation, but even then only in very small amounts. If such supplementation is necessary, remember that vitamin supplements deteriorate rapidly and therefore should be purchased in small quantities and kept in airtight, dark containers in a cool place.

Provision of good grazing pasture, or good quality grains, or sun-cured roughage which has not been stored for long periods or stored under adverse conditions, should satisfy normal requirements for vitamins. Ideally horses that are being stabled for long periods should either have access to green feed, or two to three hours' grazing each day, to ensure adequate vitamin intake, especially vitamins A and D. Alternatively a vitamin A-D supplement can be added, but daily green feed will sharpen the appetite, relieve some of the boredom, and help provide a digestive laxative.

## 6. Water.

If horses do not have an ample supply of clean, fresh water, their feed intake will be adversely affected. It is particularly important that they should have plenty of water during periods of growth, work, and lactation. The water should not be contaminated by decomposing organic matter, algae, sediments, or high salt content (maximum six grams/litre), all of which would render it unpalatable.

Water requirements vary with the type of dry matter in the diet. Allowing for the amount of rations, the amount of work, environmental temperature, stage of growth or lactation, and mineral content of the food, most horses need up to seventy litres per day. If water is not freely available and has to be provided in a container it must be remembered that household plastic buckets which are often used will hold only ten litres of water and that one or two buckets per day are not sufficient for a pony kept in a yard or stable. Either use a larger container, e.g. a small trough or an old bath, or water the pony at least three to four times each day, and even more during hot weather or periods of intensive work or training.

A horse should not be allowed to drink large quantities of water immediately after exercise, as it may cause colic. If a horse is hot and sweaty it can be given a small drink after exercise, up to two to four litres depending on the size of the horse, and allowed to walk around and cool off. After the horse has cooled off it can be allowed access to water. If a horse is being ridden continuously for more than two hours, it can be allowed a few mouthfuls of water approximately each hour depending on weather conditions.

Horses are creatures of habit. They learn by *repetition*.

## B. Examples of Supplementary Rations

These rations are based on a pony weighing 300-350 kg in weight.

The rations have been checked for calcium and phosphorus mineral balance in all cases to give a ratio of between 1.5:1 to 2.5:1 and, if the addition of a supplement is necessary, the amount to add has been calculated. The phosphorus supplement can either be sodium monophosphate (SMP—twenty-three per cent phosphorus) or sodium tripolyphosphate (STP—twenty-five per cent phosphorus) and calculations are based on adjusted availability of the mineral from each source.

### 1. Total pasture feeding.

Rations are given for both pasture and non-pasture grazing. Normally about one hectare of pasture is required to maintain a pony throughout the year, and careful attention should be given to periods of poor pasture growth or quality occurring when the feed has dried off and is fibrous and low in energy, or when it is too succulent and the pony has to eat a lot to obtain the required energy. The pasture-fed pony may need supplementation during these periods when the need is indicated by the conditions of the pony and the type of pasture.

### 2. Pasture feeding but weekend riding and pony club activities.

The pony should be able to maintain condition on good pasture alone during weekdays when the amount of exercise is limited. If the pony is given light work during the week then a suitable supplement may need to be fed to maintain the pony's condition and stamina. The ration below will supply about one-third to one-half of the pony's daily needs when grazing pasture and performing only light work. The ration is calculated to give a choice of five different ration ingredient combinations. It need be fed only once daily, and some lucerne hay may be fed at night (about 0.5-1.0 kg). If fed before going for weekend rides or pony club activities, then feed about three-quarters of the grain and half of the chaff two to three

hours before going for the ride. When the pony has cooled off after work then feed the rest. The amounts are in *kilograms* of feed unless marked as *grams* (g).

| Ingredients (kg) | Ration Alternatives | | | | |
|---|---|---|---|---|---|
| | A | B | C | D | E |
| Oaten chaff | 2.0 | 1.0 | 1.5 | 2.0 | — |
| Lucerne chaff | — | 1.0 | 0.5 | 0.5 | 2.0 |
| Oats | 1.0 | 1.0 | 1.0 | 0.7 | 0.7 |
| Bran | 200g | 200g | 200g | 200g | 200g |
| Salt | 20g | 20g | 20g | 20g | 20g |
| Molasses | — | — | — | — | 200g |
| SMP/STP | — | 20g | — | — | 30g |

### 3. Deteriorating pasture.

It will be necessary to supplement the grazing intake with some form of concentrate ration if the pasture is not supplying sufficient nutrition for the pony. The rations have been calculated for a pony performing light to medium work, or some type of daily exercise—e.g. lungeing.

The ration should be divided into equal amounts and fed at least twice or three times daily. Feed the lucerne hay with the last feed of the day. Increase the amount of supplement as the quality of the pasture decreases thus—

| Ration | Percentage of daily requirements provided by ration as pasture deteriorates. |
|---|---|
| 1 | 50% (reasonable pasture) |
| 2 | 60% (some pasture) |
| 3 | 70% (poor pasture) |
| 4 | 80% (short pasture) |
| 5 | 90% (sparse pasture) |
| 6 | 100% (no pasture, or in stable) |

| Ration 1 Ingredients (kg) | Ration Alternatives | | | | |
|---|---|---|---|---|---|
| | A | B | C | D | E |
| Oaten chaff | 1,0 | 2.0 | 1.0 | 2.0 | — |
| Lucerne chaff | 0.5 | 0.5 | 1.5 | — | 1.0 |
| Lucerne hay | 1.0 | — | — | 1.0 | 1.0 |
| Oats | 0.5 | — | 0.5 | 0.5 | 0.5 |
| Bran | 200g | 200g | 200g | — | 300g |
| Salt | 20g | 20g | 20g | 20g | 20g |
| SMP/STP | 20g | — | 20g | 20g | 20g |

| Ration 2 Ingredients (kg) | Ration Alternatives | | | | |
|---|---|---|---|---|---|
| | A | B | C | D | E |
| Oaten chaff | 2.0 | 1.0 | — | 2.0 | 1.5 |
| Lucerne chaff | 1.0 | 2.0 | 2.0 | 1.5 | |
| Lucerne hay | 1.0 | 1.0 | 1.5 | — | 1.5 |
| Oats | 0.5 | 0.5 | 0.75 | 0.5 | — |
| Bran | 200g | 200g | 200g | — | — |
| Salt | 25g | 25g | 25g | 25g | 25g |
| SMP/STP | 20g | 30g | 30g | 30g | 30g |

| Ration 3 Ingredients (kg) | Ration Alternatives | | | | |
|---|---|---|---|---|---|
| | A | B | C | D | E |
| Oaten chaff | 3.0 | 1.5 | — | 2.5 | 2.0 |
| Lucerne chaff | 1.0 | 2.5 | 2.5 | 2.5 | 2.0 |
| Lucerne hay | 1.0 | 1.0 | 2.0 | — | 1.5 |
| Oats | 0.5 | 0.5 | 0.75 | 0.5 | — |
| Bran | 300g | 300g | 300g | — | — |
| Salt | 30g | 30g | 30g | 30g | 30g |
| SMP/STP | 20g | 30g | 30g | 30g | 30g |

| Ration 4 Ingredients (kg) | Ration Alternatives | | | | |
|---|---|---|---|---|---|
| | A | B | C | D | E |
| Oaten chaff | 3.5 | 2.0 | 2.5 | 3.0 | 2.5 |
| Lucerne chaff | 1.0 | 2.5 | 1.0 | 3.0 | 1.5 |
| Lucerne hay | 1.5 | 1.5 | 2.0 | — | 1.5 |
| Oats | 0.75 | 0.75 | 1.0 | 0.75 | 1.0 |
| Bran | 300g | 300g | 300g | — | — |
| Salt | 35g | 35g | 35g | 35g | 35g |
| SMP/STP | 20g | 20g | 20g | 30g | 30g |

| Ration 5 Ingredients (kg) | Ration Alternatives | | | | |
|---|---|---|---|---|---|
| | A | B | C | D | E |
| Oaten chaff | 4.0 | 3.5 | 3.0 | 3.5 | 2.5 |
| Lucerne chaff | 1.0 | 2.0 | 1.0 | 1.5 | 2.5 |
| Lucerne hay | 1.5 | 1.5 | 2.0 | 1.5 | 1.5 |
| Oats | 1.0 | 1.0 | 1.25 | 1.25 | 1.0 |
| Bran | 400g | 400g | 400g | 400g | 200g |
| Salt | 40g | 40g | 40g | 40g | 40g |
| SMP/STP | 20g | 20g | 20g | 20g | 30g |

| Ration 6 Ingredients (kg) | Ration Alternatives | | | | |
|---|---|---|---|---|---|
| | A | B | C | D | E |
| Oaten chaff | 4.5 | 4.0 | 3.5 | 4.0 | 3.0 |
| Lucerne chaff | 1.0 | 1.5 | 1.5 | — | 2.0 |
| Lucerne hay | 1.5 | 1.5 | 2.0 | 2.5 | 1.5 |
| Oats | 1.0 | 1.25 | 1.5 | 1.5 | 1.0 |
| Bran | 400g | 300g | 400g | 300g | 400g |
| Salt | 45g | 45g | 45g | 45g | 45g |
| SMP/STP | 20g | 20g | 20g | — | 20g |

## Remember

• if the pony is losing weight—deworm for parasites, check teeth, etc., before increasing ration.

• if the pony is developing a 'hay belly'—decrease the roughage and increase the oat content, but balance the ration with appropriate exercise so that the pony does not become too energetic or hard to handle.

• if the pony is gaining weight—decrease the overall ration amount.

• when feeding ration 6—if possible provide some greenfeed (about 1 kg), e.g. fresh lucerne, grass, etc., at least twice a week to sharpen the appetite, but not lawn clippings.

• if the pony is being trained for eventing or endurance riding—use the above rations for ponies doing light to medium work and increase the energy level in the ration by increasing the oat supplement for each ration by 0.5 to 1 kg. Keep a close watch on the condition and stamina of the pony and adjust accordingly. Molasses can be used either in the liquid form, as a 50:50 mixture in warm water and mixed into the feed, or in the powdered form, and can be substituted on a weight and approximate energy-value basis, but should only constitute a maximum of ten per cent of the ration. Other energy supplements such as corn, wheat, and barley can be used also. The salt levels can be increased by 10 g per ration to ensure adequate provision for the increased work.

• if a shiny coat with good lustre ('bloom') is required—30 g of polyunsaturated oil (such as safflower, corn, cottonseed, coconut, or peanut oil) can be added to the ration to accomplish this. Add the oil immediately before feeding, as the food mix may turn rancid if prepared too early. This addition will not affect the nutritive value of the ration to any great extent. The use of polyunsaturated oil is suggested instead of the usual addition of linseed meal which is high in fibre and low in digestibility and quality and therefore would increase the roughage content of the ration.

• if oats are not available—the following grain

substitutes can be used, taking oats as a standard for energy value:

1 kg oats can be replaced    0.8 kg barley
            by               0.75 kg corn
                             0.9 kg corn on cob
                             0.85 kg sorghum
                             0.8 kg wheat

These grains are best fed either crimped, cracked, or coarsely crushed. Although usually they can be safely fed instead of oats, many owners mix them on a 50:50 energy-value basis with oats to give a basically open digestive mass with little digestive upset.

## EXERCISE

All horses require some exercise to ensure good health and active digestion. This is especially important in stabled horses or horses confined to small yards, and ten to twenty minutes of exercise daily in the form of lungeing, riding, or training is the least that should be done, especially if high-energy rations are being fed. This may prevent the horse becoming excessively fat, difficult to handle, or suffering digestive upsets.

The grazing horse at rest will usually exercise itself sufficiently during grazing to maintain reasonable health.

A yearling standing in the ideal pose to be shown or photographed

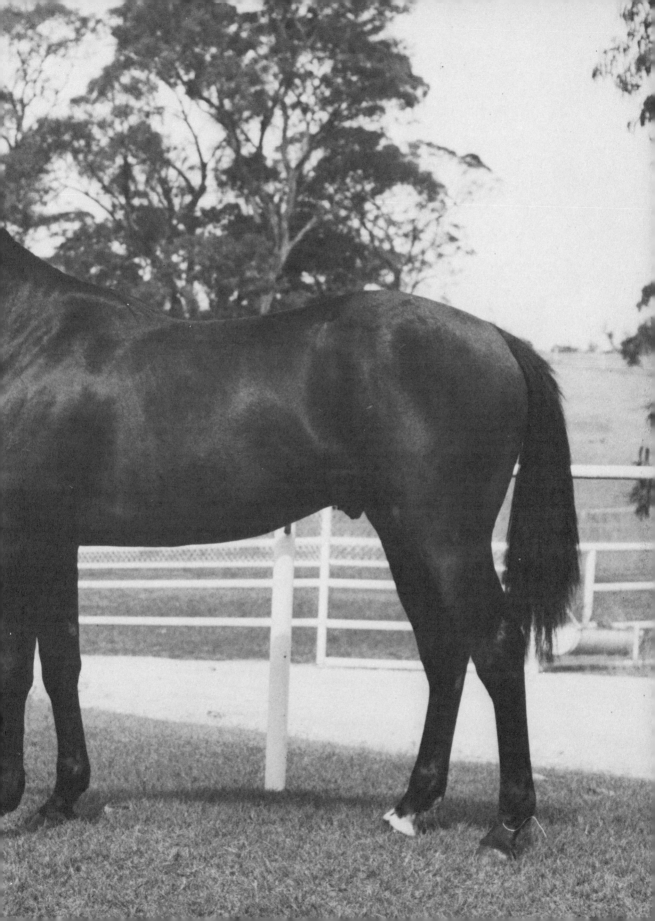

# 11

# First Aid

## FIRST AID FOR HORSES

Horses are accident prone. Because of their speed, size, and spirited behaviour they have a habit of galloping into fences, getting caught up in wire, or injuring themselves while playing. They are easily frightened and, in their speed to escape, can hurt themselves very badly. They are also very inquisitive, and this, too, can lead to injury.

It is important to be familiar with the principle of first aid, including how to arrest bleeding, clean and dress wounds, and how to calm the horse.

Horses should be vaccinated against tetanus at an early age and receive booster injections from time to time, especially after serious injury. Contact a veterinary surgeon for more knowledge about a vaccination course and routine.

### A SIMPLE FIRST-AID KIT

A small first-aid kit can be made up for a few dollars and it should be kept handy (near tack room perhaps) for *emergency only*. Carry a kit in the float with the horse, because injuries occur during or after travelling.

Some suggestions for the contents are listed:

1 x small roll of cotton wool.
1 x roll of adhesive bandage (7.5 - 10 cm wide).

1 x small bottle of antiseptic solution such as Cetavlon ®, Hibitane ®, Zepharin ®, Savlon ®, etc.
1 x small pair of 15 cm scissors with blunt ends.
1 x small jar of petroleum jelly (optional).
1 x 7.5 - 10 cm wide x 2 m long linen or cloth bandage to use as a constriction bandage, with a large safety pin (napkin pin).
1 x 7.5 - 10 cm wide roll of gauze bandage.

## TREATMENTS

### WOUNDS
#### 1. Arrest the bleeding
*For Wounds below the Elbow or Hock*

Degree 1. *If small blood vessels* are bleeding, they should clot and cease to bleed in from five

Minimum requirements in a first-aid kit

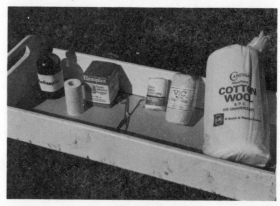

to ten minutes. These wounds will normally only involve layers of skin. Treat with surface antibiotic powders or sprays and make sure the wound is kept clean.

Degree 2. *If large blood vessels* are bleeding apply a pressure bandage to prevent blood loss. These will usually be confined to skin and muscle layers. It should be possible to remove the pressure bandage in from one to two hours.

*Method*

1. Quickly smear a thin layer of petroleum jelly around the wound (optional). This will help prevent the pads sticking to the skin around the wound and it will be very easy to remove the pad.

2. Cut the gauze bandage into small double-layer folded swabs (10 cm x 10 cm) and place these over the wound, hold in place with fingers.

3. Place a 1.5 cm thick layer of cotton wool over the swabs.

4. Wrap one or two layers of adhesive bandage or cotton gauze around the cotton wool pad and extend the bandage about 5 cm above the pad to hold it in place.

Degree 3. *If very large blood vessels* are bleeding, indicated by spurting of blood, etc., wrap

Place pad over the wound and hold it in place with the fingers

*To apply a pressure pad and bandage:*

Cut gauze into small double-folded swabs large enough to cover the wound, or use a clean piece of cotton material. Put a backing of 2-cm thick cotton wool on to the swab

If on a limb the pad can be held in place with a bandage. Wrap a thin layer of cotton wool around the leg and over the pad

Wrap one or two layers of cotton gauze or adhesive bandage around the limb over a pad

Extend the bandage 5 cm above the pad area to hold it in place. Secure with an adhesive bandage or a knotted bandage

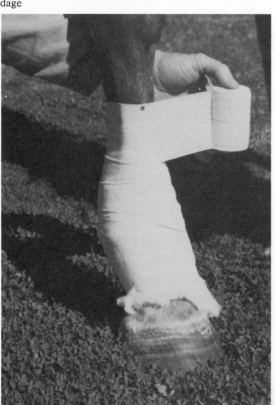

the constrictive bandage several times very tightly around the leg above the wound and secure it in place with the safety pin. Release the constrictive bandage for about one minute in every fifteen minutes.

As well, repeat steps 1-4 above — using a thicker layer of cotton wool to absorb more blood.

*For Wounds of the Body or Head*

Similar principles for degrees 1 to 3, but hold the pad in place with hand.

## 2. Calm the horse

This will usually be necessary in cases of large wounds or when the horse is excited or severely stressed.

Talk to the horse quietly, rub or stroke him

*To apply a constrictive bandage (leg wounds only):*

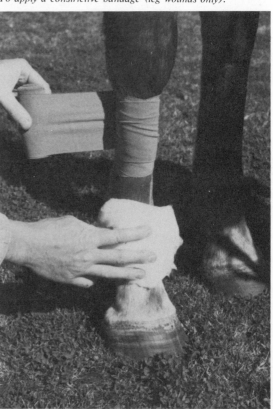

Tightly wrap a 2-metre long by 7.5 cm-to-10 cm wide cotton, elastic gauze, or linen bandage around the leg above the wound

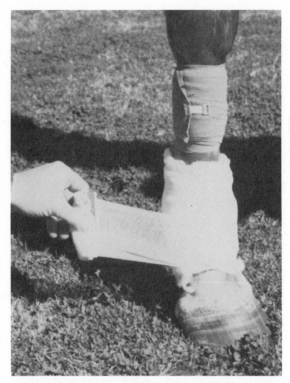

Secure in place with an adhesive bandage or safety pin. Apply a pressure pad to the wound. Release the constrictive bandage in 15 minutes. Reapply after one minute if the wound still bleeds through the pressure pad

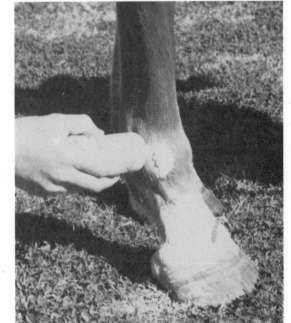

Apply antibiotic or dressing lotions to the wound

on the neck, don't move quickly in his vicinity and, if possible, take him into a quiet, darkened stall or loose box.

After the bleeding has been arrested, offer the horse a drink of cool, clean water from a shallow bucket and some palatable feed such as fresh green feed to help settle him down and aid his recovery.

The horse should also be made as comfortable as possible. Move to a sheltered area, if possible, and rug him and provide adequate feed and water. If he is injured outside and cannot be safely moved, put a rug on him to keep him warm—especially if it is cold and wet.

### 3. Clean the wound
After the bleeding has ceased, carefully inspect the wound for foreign bodies adhering to or embedded in it. If they are very deeply embedded in the wound a veterinary surgeon should be called to remove them under appropriate sedation and anaesthetic. These include bullets, broken-off stakes, metal, glass, wire, etc.

Clean the wound by lightly squirting or trickling a saline solution (one teaspoon of salt in half-a-litre of boiled water) into the wound. If this saline is unavailable, then cold running water from a hose can be trickled into the wound. This will remove hair, blood clots, etc.

Disinfect the wound by trickling a 1 in 1000 solution of antiseptic solution and water into it.

Large wounds may be best left covered by the pressure bandage until inspected by a veterinary surgeon.

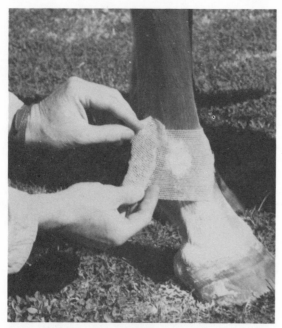

Place a gauze pad or paraffin gauze pad over the wound

Wrap a thin layer (1 cm) of cotton wool around the leg

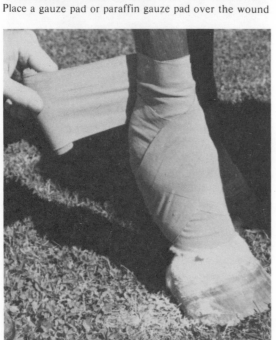

Firmly, but not tightly, wrap a gauze, elastic crêpe, or elastic adhesive bandage over the cotton wool, extending 5 cm above and below the wound area

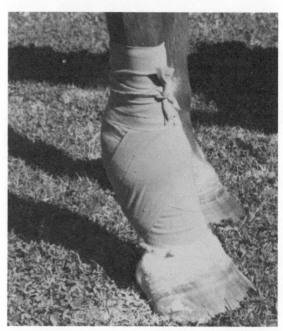

Secure with an elastic adhesive bandage or a knotted bandage

## 4. Dress the wound

Once the wound is cleaned, dress it with anti-biotic powder or cream if any is available and apply bandage if necessary to keep it clean. Larger wounds should be dressed by a veterinary surgeon.

## FRACTURES

If a horse obviously fractures a long bone of the leg, calm him down and ring a veterinary surgeon for advice. If a severe knock or kick to a bony structure results in rapid swelling, dis-alignment, or pain, it may be possible to sup-port the injured limb by applying a thick layer of cotton wool covered by a firm (but not tight) bandage until the veterinary surgeon arrives.

## BRUISES KICKS, FALLS, OVERREACH-ING

1. Arrest any bleeding.
2. Hose down area with cold running water for ten to fifteen minutes to help reduce the swelling and pain, or place an ice pack over the site, and walk the horse if possible as this will help to reduce some of the swelling.
3. Bandage appropriately with a supporting bandage if necessary, repeat hosing for ten to twenty minutes twice daily until swelling decreases. Consult a veterinary surgeon if the horse becomes or remains lame or excessive swelling develops, or if the injury is particularly severe.

## SNAKE BITE

Although the severity of snake bite depends on the location of the bite, the thickness of the skin, the speed of the horse, and the species of snake (and therefore may not be harmful to the horse) it is best to take precautionary action. Snake bites often cause bad infections at the site of the bite, due to highly contaminated teeth, and cleaning the wound is essential.

1. Wash the area with clean, cold, running water as soon as possible to wash off the surface venom and thus help to decrease the amount of poison absorbed into the system, and clean the wound.
2. If the bite is in a limb, apply a constrictive bandage around the limb above the bite.

Release the bandage around the limb for one minute every twenty minutes to avoid limb necrosis. However, the poison may spread at this time.

3. Try to identify the snake. Contact a veterinary surgeon to advise the species so that appropiate antivenene can be given.

## BURNS, SCALDS

1. Remove cause if practical—in cases of electric shock do not approach the horse until the power is turned off.
2. Minor burns (such as rope burns)—wash liberally with cold water or press on an ice pack to reduce heat and pain.
3. Wash the burn with a dilute solution of saline (one teaspoon of salt in half a litre of boiled water), Cetavlon ®, Zepharin ®, etc. —sponge lightly to clean and dry.
4. Apply a suitable burn cream, such as Ungvita ®, Dibrogan ®, etc. Do not apply butter or similar substances.
5. Dress areas with a clean gauze swab and bandage to keep the area clean.
6. Contact a veterinary surgeon for advice.

## POISONS

1. If the poisonous substance or plant (e.g. oleander) is eaten, try to identify it, or collect a sample and contact a veterinary surgeon immediately.
2. If one horse in a paddock of horses is affected by suspected food or water poisoning, remove all other horses from the area and collect similar samples.
3. If a corrosive substance, such as a strong acid or alkali, is spilt on the horse's skin, wash off the substance immediately with cold, running water. Alkalis (e.g. lime) can be neutralised by a solution of 1:1 vinegar and water. Acids can be neutralised by a solution of one dessertspoon of baking soda (sodium bicarbonate) in half a litre of warm water. Both should be liberally applied to the affected area.
4. Contact a veterinary surgeon for advice.

## COLIC

1. Colic has many causes, including grain engorgement, sand ingestion, bowel twists or impactions, and digestive upsets.
2. Walk the animal to keep it on its feet,

don't allow it to roll, and don't allow access to feed or water.

3. Contact a veterinary surgeon as soon as possible for an accurate diagnosis. Many home remedies are not beneficial for certain causes of colic.

## EYE WOUNDS

1. Try to calm the horse if it is very excited.

2. Assess the injury and contact a veterinary surgeon for advice.

3. If the horse is obviously affected by light, either blindfold him, if he will tolerate it, or take him to a darkened area.

## WASP STINGS OR SEVERE BEE STINGS

Horses can sometimes be attacked by swarms of bees and be stung severely. If stung many times around the head and neck the resultant swelling can cause suffocation or severe shock.

1. Calm the horse.

2. Remove the stings by carefully scraping out sideways to remove the major portion of the poison bag.

3. Apply a solution of baking soda (one dessertspoon of baking soda in half a litre of warm water).

4. Call a veterinary surgeon immediately for advice.

5. Apply antihistamine or local anaesthetic creams, if available, as these may be valuable in reducing the swelling and pain.

## AZOTURIA

Azoturia sometimes takes a mild form of 'tying up', and is also called Monday morning sickness, blackwater, or paralytic myoglobinuria. Usually it is associated with exercise after a period of inactivity or rest when a high grain diet has not been restricted during the rest period.

The symptoms are rapid heart rate, sweating, muscular stiffness and pain, especially in the hindquarters, and often in severe cases the passing of brown/black urine. Signs develop after exercise, which need not be vigorous, from fifteen to sixty minutes after commencement.

Ponies or hacks receiving little or no weekly exercise may develop symptoms if ridden or exercised more than usual on weekends.

The horse should be given complete rest — definitely no more exercise — or severe muscular damage may occur. Keep the horse standing and as warm and quiet as possible. If the horse is sweating profusely rub him dry, and in cold weather put a rug on him.

Care for the horse on the spot; provide shelter if necessary. If he has to be moved then take him home in a float or trailer and restrict him to a warm loose box. Reduce the horse's food intake to a maintenance diet with a minimum of grain, but allow access to water. In severe cases a veterinary surgeon should be contacted immediately for advice and treatment to avoid extreme muscle degeneration or death.

Often a warm bran mash containing sixty grams of bicarbonate of soda (baking soda) acts as a laxative and helps to decrease the acidic metabolite level in the blood; feed this twice daily. A bran mash is made as follows: scald one kilogram of bran in a bucket with boiling water, stirring to achieve a wet but not sloppy mixture. Mix in ten grams (two teaspoons) of salt. Cover the bucket with a bag and allow the mash to cool before feeding.

## LAMINITIS

This is also called 'founder' or 'heat in the feet'. It is the name for inflammation of the sensitive layers in the hooves.

Although there are a lot of causes the most common is the intake of higher quantities than normal of rich protein feeds, which can occur in horses engorging grain, or in ponies receiving little or no exercise on spring pastures. These ponies often develop deformities of the feet. Mares that fail to expel their afterbirth completely, or horses receiving sudden bursts of hard work, can also develop founder.

Horses standing for long periods, e.g. during transport or because of leg injuries, or horses suffering from some infectious diseases, may be subject to founder. Ingestion of large quantities of cold water by an over-hot horse can also lead to founder. At times all four feet can be affected, but usually only the front feet show signs.

It is recognised by sweating, muscle twitching, acute lameness, and at times by all four feet placed forward of their normal upright position to the extent that the horse is able to stand on his heels. Movement is very painful and slow. When the coronary band is pressed lightly the horse feels extreme pain and the feet feel hot. At times the hoof can be shed, or its shape can be radically altered, and the horse remains permanently lame.

First aid is helpful but a veterinary surgeon should be contacted immediately, as there are many causes and treatments differ for each cause.

1. Stand the horse in cold water (e.g. a dam, creek, or artificial mud hole); hose down the feet with cold water; or apply ice poultices to the affected feet (in a plastic bag wrapped around the feet) for thirty minutes at a time to reduce the pain and inflammation.

2. Keep the horse blanketed in cold weather.

3. Make the horse walk for thirty minutes if possible between each cold-water treatment. If the horse is unable to walk, alternate cold soaking and hot soaking (not boiling, but hot enough for the hand to be immersed and then have to be withdrawn) for thirty minutes each may aid recovery.

4. Remove possible cause, e.g. stop access to grain, etc.

5. Reduce diet to dry feed or chaff.

6. A laxative bran mash fed twice daily (see preparation of bran mash as described in Azoturia) may be helpful in founder due to excessive intake of higher protein foods (grain engorgement, etc.) but contact a veterinary surgeon for additional treatment.

Record the local veterinary surgeon or hospital's name and address in the space provided below: _____

Dr . . . . . . . . . . . . . . . . . . . . . . . . . . . . . . . . . .

Address . . . . . . . . . . . . . . . . . . . . . . . . . . . . . . .

Telephone No. (Business) . . . . . . . . . . . . . . . .

(After Hours) . . . . . . . . . . . . .

**Essential items to prepare for a veterinary surgeon's visit**
1. A bucket of clean warm water.
2. A cake of soap.
3. A clean towel.
4. A note pad to record treatments, etc.
5. A cup of coffee and a smile!

Simple requirements for a veterinarian's visit

# POSSIBLE PROBLEM AREAS OF THE HORSE

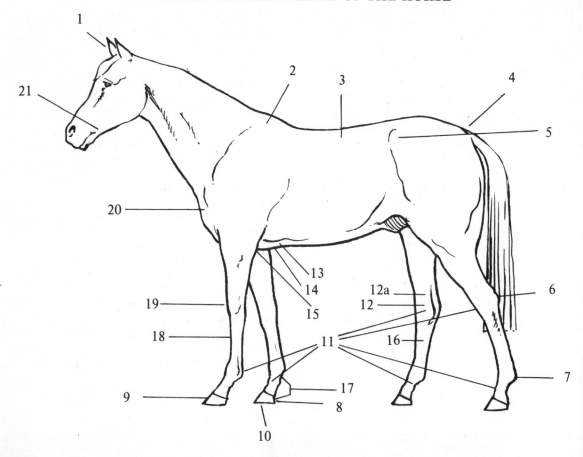

| PROBLEM. | COMMONLY CAUSED BY. |
|---|---|
| 1. Abscess in ears. | Ear mite infestation. |
| 2. Sore wither. | Ill-fitting saddle, tight-fitting saddlecloth, ill-fitting rug. |
| 3. Sore back. | Ill-fitting saddle, weight of rider too far back. |
| 4. Sore under dock. | Tight and/or abrasive crupper. |
| 5. Damage to point of hip. | Allowing horse to hit side of door or gate opening. |
| 6. Capped hock. | Kicking solid object. |
| 7. Bruising and damage to ergot area (Stoppers). | Area striking ground. |
| 8. Gashed heels. | Hind foot striking heel (overreaching). |
| 9. Cracked, split hoof. | Dry conditions. |

| | |
|---|---|
| 10. Sore feet. | Bruising, insufficient horn, etc. |
| 11. Damage and bruising. | Brushing and/or knocking. Irregular gait. |
| 12. Bog Spavin. ⎱ | |
| 12a. Thorough Pin. ⎰ | Stress and/or conformation fault. |
| 13. Galls | Girth. |
| 14. Swelling in girth area. | Reaction to narrow, tight girth. |
| 15. Sores under armpit. | Martingale strap chafing when not central-ised between forelegs. Girth galls compli-cated by infection. |
| 16. Speedy cutting. | Heel of foreshoe striking this area. |
| 17. Lacerations and bruising. | Hind foot striking this area. |
| 18. Splint. | Damage, stress, or strain. |
| 19. Lacerated knee. | Stumbling, slippery surface, etc. |
| 20 Loss of hair on shoulder. | Chafing of ill-fitting rug. |
| 21. Associated with the head area. | Teething. |
| | Sharp edges of teeth. |
| | Lacerated cheek linings. |
| | Lacerated cheek exterior. |
| | Lacerated tongue. |
| | Chafed lips (sore mouth). |
| | Bruising to interior of mouth. |
| | Plant seeds imbedded in mouth. |
| | Abnormal development. |
| | Sore on facial crest, due to headcollar, etc., rubbing. |
| | Damage to eye, causing restricted vision. |

Azoturia and muscular tying-up symp-toms. Stiffness and hardening of muscles, cramped action, coupled with reluctance to move.

Excess work after a period of little or no exer-cise, often coupled with a high-energy diet.

# Appendix I

### THE FARRIER

The farrier should be summoned if he has not paid a visit to inspect and trim the young horse's feet by the time he is six months old. The farrier can correct and advise on the treatment of any abnormalities that may be becoming apparent. Prompt attention at this stage can guide the formation of the young horse's foot into a sound and shapely appendage.

The horse should be thoroughly familiar with the raising and handling of his feet long before the farrier has to carry out his duties. It is unfair to the farrier to have to effect on-the-spot education lessons. He is there to treat the foot, not to initiate education to the horse. Beside which, a hurried and ineffectual lesson is certainly not in the best interests or safety of the horse.

Another point is that a young horse should always be held by a competent person who has the confidence of the horse and is aware of the correct method of holding the horse, in order to ensure the maximum safety of the farrier.

*The following five photographs show the farrier inducing the young horse to raise his near hind leg.*

18.  The horse has been positioned correctly by the handler. The weight of the horse is distributed in such a manner that the raising of the near side hind will not cause the horse to move in order to keep his balance. The farrier's left hand is in firm contact with the point of the hip. The handler should stand on the same side of the horse as the farrier

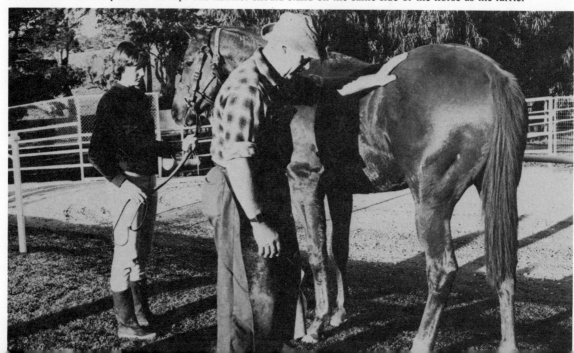

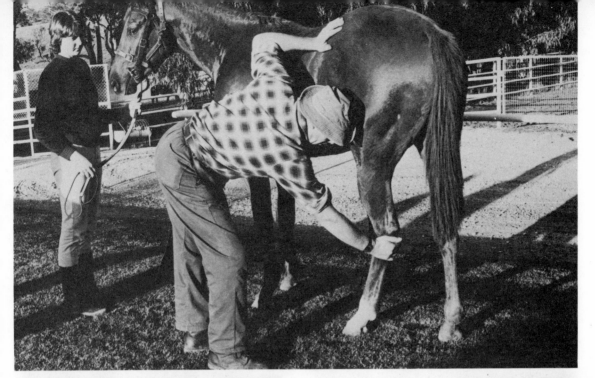

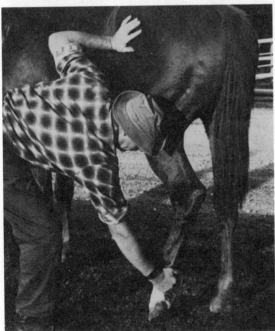

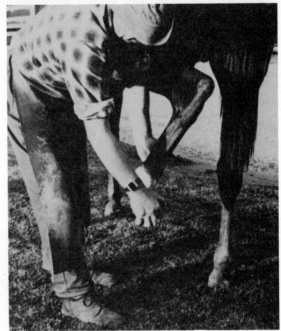

19.   *Top:* Contact with the right hand is made at the point of the hip adjacent to the left hand. Maintaining contact, the right hand is moved down the rear of the leg

20.   *Above, left:* The right hand is moved down to the pastern. Pressure from the left hand assists in removing the weight from the leg

21.   *Above, right:* As soon as the foot is raised the right hand is slid over the base of the foot. Many young horses will accept the hand on the foot rather than on a joint. The action of the left hand is important, as it illustrates familiarising the horse with contact to the front of the cannon bone

22.  The cannon bone is the area that is in contact with the farrier's hip when the leg is placed in readiness for work on the foot

The professional approach to this segment of the youngster's education is shown in the photographs numbered 18, 19, 20, 21, and 22. Not only is the farrier transmitting signals to the horse in order to effect a response but also the horse is giving signals as to his rate of acceptance through the movements of his muscles, head, eyes, ears, etc. Even though these movements may be very small the handler or trainer should learn to interpret the signals, as they are virtually a language of their own.

102

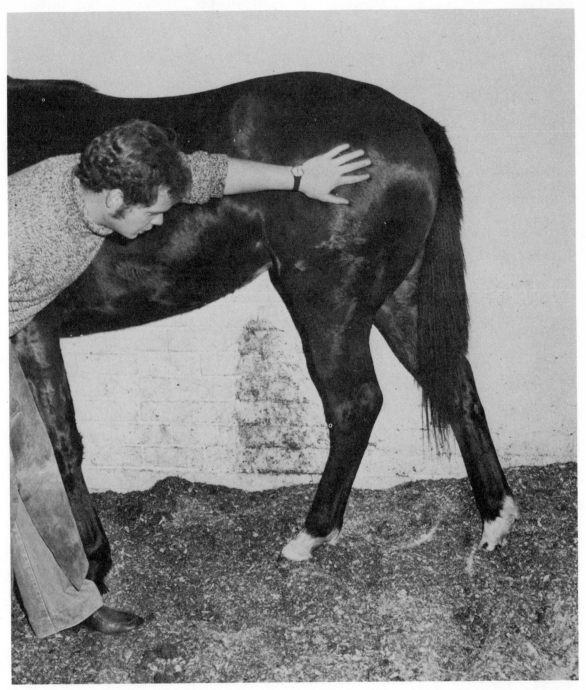

23.  In raising and holding the hind leg of a confirmed or potential kicker only one hand is used but continuous contact with the horse is maintained by the farrier's side and back

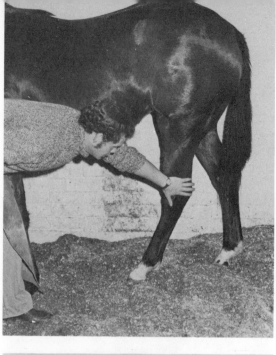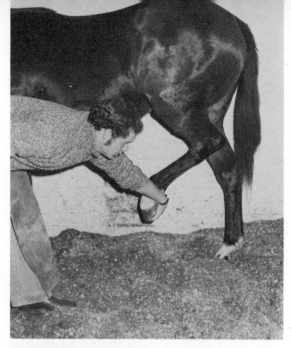

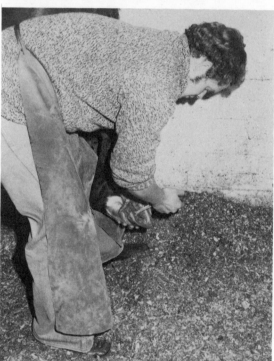

24. *Top, left:* Positioning of the horse by the handler at the horse's head is important in ensuring that the leg to be raised is not bearing a great amount of weight

25. *Top, right:* The foot is not raised to conventional height for a few lessons

26. *Above, left:* The foot is kept low

27. *Above, right:* The horse accepts the procedure willingly

# Appendix II

## FIRE BRANDING

In those countries where fire branding is required for identification and stud book purposes, etc., it is best done at the weanling age, remembering that the brand must be clean and level, red hot, and, preferably, the area in which the brand is to be applied is clipped of excess hair. If the brand is red hot (not to melting point) it need only be applied for a few seconds for the required impression. Longer contact has to be made when the brand is less than red hot, thus increasing the risk of skin movement and smudging.

The horse must be held perfectly still in an enclosed area such as a horse box. A great aid to successful branding is a nose twitch which produces a numbing effect on the upper lip, and yet no great discomfort to the horse. It effectively restrains the animal from moving.

Taking care not to be over-vigorous, twitching is carried out by grasping the upper lip and, after placing the twitch loop over it, twisting firmly without damaging the lip. This is only to be applied for a short period, as circulation can cease and the twitch lose any effect that has occurred.

The twitch should not be used abusively, but must be applied with caution; also taking care not to stand in front of the animal but alongside the shoulder. A hand covering the youngster's eye will prevent him from seeing the brand approaching and thus eliminate flinching. For application of the twitch refer to colour photo 30. When the twitch is used in conjunction with a headcollar and lead rein it is a good policy to wrap two half hitches of the lead rein around the twitch handle, thus making it more secure. The twitch loop can be attached to a handle as shown, or to a metal ring.

While on the subject of identification, the story is told of two simple people who loved to go riding together but were always disagreeing over who owned which horse. A brilliant idea occurred to one rider. If he cut a nick in his horse's ear they would be able to tell them apart.

All went well for a week and there was no disagreement. But then the other horse caught his head in a wire fence and nicked his ear, too.

Disagreements again followed over which horse was whose. Another brilliant idea occurred to the brighter of the two riders: cut a portion off the bottom of one horse's tail.

Peace followed for another week or so, until the other horse's tail caught in the fence and a portion was pulled off.

Further disagreement followed until a really clever idea occurred to the not-quite-so-bright rider: they should measure the height of the horses. When they did so all was well, for they found that the grey horse was definitely one hand higher than the black horse.

# Appendix III

## REARING ORPHAN FOALS

A foal becomes an orphan when the mare dies during or soon after foaling, when its mother rejects it, or when the mare produces insufficient quantities of milk—especially when there are twins. Occasionally a mare may be slow to 'let down' her milk. Consult a veterinary surgeon in this case. An injection of hormone may be necessary to allow her to feed her foal the first time.

Orphans can be foster-mothered or reared by hand.

*Importance of colostrum milk*
If the foal has not sucked at all, colostrum (or first milk) should be fed. Foals that do not receive colostrum often show poor disease resistance and growth rates. Colostrum contains antibodies that give the foal protection against diseases with which the mare has come in contact, or for which she has received recent vaccinations or booster injections against. Colostrum also contains high-quality protein, minerals, and vitamins. It is easily digested and contains a natural laxative.

Sources of colostrum are: another mare which has recently foaled—within forty-eight hours of foaling; a mare that has had a dead foal (although it would be better for such a mare to foster-mother the orphan immedi-

*Facing page:* Two bit rings of the eggbutt snaffle are shown joined by means of a link rein attached to the lead

ately); the orphan's own dead mother—if she died in labour or soon after birth from a non-infectious disease, and if the colostrum is collected immediately; frozen colostrum stores; and artificial colostrum.

*Collection of colostrum*
Colostrum must be collected under hygienic conditions to avoid gastric upsets in the recipient foals.

Usually the source is a mare with plenty of milk that has foaled within the previous forty-eight hours. Her own foal must be kept from sucking for about one hour if possible.

The method of collecting colostrum is:
1. Carefully and gently wash the mare's udder and teats with warm, soapy water (e.g. Velvet® soap). Wash from the near side with a hand on the mare's rump to lessen the chance of being kicked. The person holding the mare should stand on the same side and talk to her soothingly. If the mare becomes excited, back her into a corner and hold the near side front leg off the ground while washing. The use of a twitch is usually not necessary.
2. Rinse the udder with clean, warm water.
3. Make sure your hands are clean.
4. Gently strip out the first few drops of colostrum from each teat.
5. Milk the teats, collecting the colostrum in a sterilised container. Collect as much as possible.

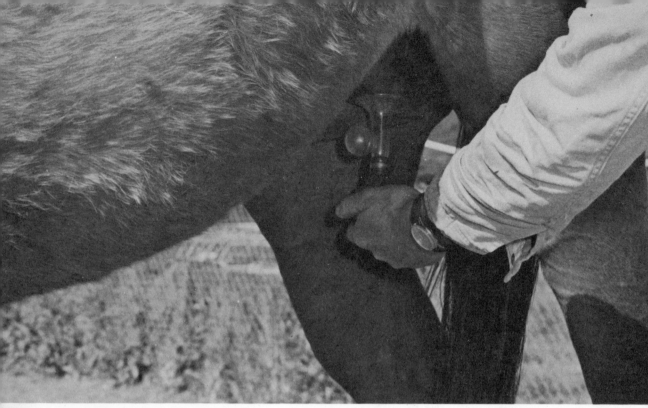

Use a human breast pump to milk a mare quickly and easily

6. Wash the udder with clean, cold water and dry with a clean, disposable towel or tissue.

Colostrum can be kept in a refrigerator for from one to two days. Long-term storage in a freezer is worthwhile for later orphan foal emergencies. Store the colostrum in a container (about three-quarters full) after it has been well sealed and labelled.

### Feeding colostrum

Freshly collected colostrum can be fed directly to the orphan using a sterilised cool-drink bottle and a large rubber calf teat about 8 cm long. Teats are available from stock agents and chemists.

The teat hole may have to be enlarged to enable the thick colostrum to pass through. Ideally, a drop should emerge through the teat hole when the bottle is held upside down. Frozen colostrum should be gently heated in warm water to blood heat (39°C) before feeding.

The method of feeding the colostrum is: Wet the feeding teat with colostrum. Hold the teat on the bottle firmly to prevent the foal pulling it off while sucking. Tempt the foal to start sucking. Allow the foal to drink as much as he wants. Repeat the process every two hours. (See Table for details of colostrum feeding.)

If initial restraint is necessary, embrace the foal gently from the side with the arms around and under the neck and tail while someone manipulates the bottle.

When fresh or frozen colostrum is not available, artificial colostrum can be formulated. Mix the formula daily and store it in a refrigerator between feeds. Contact a veterinary surgeon for advice about an injection of 'hyper-immune' horse serum to make sure the foal receives his antibodies.

A formula for artificial colostrum:
1000 ml of cow's milk
1 beaten egg (supplies protein)
20 ml of cod liver oil (optional)
40 g brown sugar (supplies energy)
20 ml paraffin oil (acts as a laxative)
If the foal scours, cease paraffin addition.

108

## The hand-rearing process

If a foster-mother is not available hand rearing will be necessary and this requires a great deal of care.

Milk formulas are based on cow's milk or proprietary milk replacers (e.g. Denkavit®). Mare's milk contains more water and sugar than cow's milk and both formula bases have to have these two components added to approximate mare's milk.

The availability of the type of milk will determine the choice. Powdered milk replacers are easy to store. Mix thoroughly in clean water each feed. Low butterfat cow's milk—for example, Friesian milk—is ideal, but make sure it is not sour.

*Formula suggestions based on cow's milk:*

### A.

1000 ml cow's milk
300 ml limewater*
60 g lactose (preferable), brown sugar, or molasses

* Mix 5 g of agricultural lime in one litre of cooled, boiled water. Allow to settle overnight. Pour off and use liquid.

### B.

1000 ml cow's milk
300 ml warm water
60 g lactose (preferable), brown sugar, or molasses
60 g potassium bicarbonate

*Formula suggestion based on milk replacers:*

### C.

1000 ml of milk replacer made up to manufacturer's directions
60 g lactose (preferable), brown sugar, or molasses

*Feeding suggestions based on thoroughbred-size foals:*

| Age of foal | Mixture | Frequency of feeding | Amount per feed (approx.) | Additions |
|---|---|---|---|---|
| 0 to 72 hours | fresh colostrum, frozen colostrum, artificial colostrum | every 2 hours 6 a.m. to 10 p.m. once at 2 a.m. | 500 ml | — |
| Remainder of first week | formula A, B, or C | 4-hourly 6 a.m. to 10 p.m. (5 feeds) | 750 to 1000 ml | clean water |
| Second week | formula A, B, or C | 4-hourly (5 feeds) | 1000 to 1500 ml | clean water |
| Third week | formula A, B, or C | 5-hourly (4 feeds) | 1500 to 2000 ml | clean water, green pasture |
| Fourth week | formula A, B, or C with or without sugar | 5-hourly (4 feeds) | 2000 to 2500 ml | clean water, green pasture, mix of 3:1 crushed oats and bran as supplement |
| Fifth week | cow's milk with 200 ml water, milk replacer | 6-hourly, 3 feeds— morning, noon, and evening | 2500 to 3000 ml | as above |
| Sixth week | cow's milk, milk replacer | 6-hourly | 3 to 4 litres | as above (skim milk can be fed if foal eating above supplements), lucerne hay |
| Eighth week | cow's milk, milk replacer | morning and evening | 4 to 5 litres | as above |
| Tenth week to 4 months | cow's milk, milk replacer | morning and evening | 4 to 5 litres | clean water, good pasture, lucerne hay, 3:1 crushed oats-bran mix |
| After 4 months | cow's milk, milk replacer, or begin weaning process | once daily | 4 to 5 litres | as above |
| 5 months | weaning process (see below) | — | — | weaning rations |

Cleanliness of utensils is vital, especially in the early stages, to avoid gastric upsets and diarrhoea.

Wash bottles, teats, and buckets with clean cold water after use and wash utensils in a warm detergent solution once daily to remove grease and other deposits.

Sanitise utensils in boiling water or suitable cold sanitiser before feeding. Soaking utensils in solutions of Milton® or dairy iodophor is good practice between feeds. It is inexpensive, easy, less time consuming, and at times more efficient than boiling utensils. Follow the directions on the bottle for Milton®.

Change from bottle feeding to bucket feeding within the first week or so.

Put milk in a wide, shallow container in a small enclosure with the orphan. Show the foal where the milk is and splash milk on his nose. Leave the foal alone—he will usually start drinking once he becomes hungry.

A shallow plastic bucket 30 cm in diameter, 20 cm to 25 cm deep secured 60 cm above the ground is ideal to prevent the foal standing in it, tipping it over, or fouling it. Automatic foal-feeding units are available for groups of orphan foals.

Weak foals need special nursing in a warm loose box or room. Warmth is most important; clean straw or hay bedding is a good example.

Shelter from wind and rain is important for the first two to three weeks. Outside yards should be well drained, sheltered from prevailing winds, spelled regularly, and contain good green pasture if possible. Keep the yards clean; a half-hectare to one hectare size is ideal. Fences must be injury proof (e.g. no barbed wire).

Allow access to clean water at all times.

An orphan should have a companion animal to prevent fretting, poor feeding, or becoming a nuisance by demanding too much human attention. Another foal is best; however, if that is not possible, use a quiet old pony, a small calf, an old ewe, or a couple of pet lambs. Provide separate feeding utensils.

Certain rules of feeding should be observed to prevent gastric upsets, diarrhoea, or food refusal. Changes in diet must be made gradually. The earliest feeds should be offered at blood heat (39°C). After three days this can gradually be lowered to room temperature. Change formulas over two to three days, and do not over-feed.

Newly-born foals should pass their first dung or 'meconium' after their first feed. If the foal strains for a time without passing meconium, seek veterinary advice.

If a foal scours badly it may die of dehydration or infection.

Over-feeding and sudden changes in milk temperature or composition can cause scouring. Contaminated yards, dirty utensils, and lack of general hygiene can cause severe bacterial scours. If the foal has a temperature above 40°C, has evil-smelling or blood-stained scours, loses its appetite, and is listless, suspect bacterial scours and seek veterinary advice as soon as possible. If the foal still has a good appetite, is bright and alert with a not unpleasant smelling scour, shift him to a clean area, reduce the amount of milk in the diet, and offer clean water. Dose with 100 to 200 g of plain flour paste or 50 ml of Kaomagma®. If the scour persists for more than twenty-four to thirty-six hours, or the foal becomes dehydrated (the skin when pinched up returns to its normal position slowly) or listless, seek veterinary advice.

Ensure that the foal has a sufficient area to exercise and receive at least two to three hours of sunlight a day, preferably more. The foal should be taught to lead as soon as possible.

At two months of age the foal can be treated for worms with a paste formulation; repeat the worming every two months, shifting to a new pasture after each deworming if possible.

Although successful weaning can be done as early as four months, it is best to wean at five to six months of age. Gradually reduce the amount of milk offered at each feed over about one week. Wean on to green pasture if possible, with supplements and good-quality lucerne hay.

A suitable weaning supplement is:

| | |
|---|---|
| lucerne chaff | 1.5 kg |
| oats | 1.0 kg |
| soya bean meal | 0.75 kg |
| molasses | 0.25 kg |
| calcium diphosphate | 70 g |
| salt | 15 g |

Feed this supplement daily. It gives good protein, 70 per cent of daily nutrient requirements, and has a balanced calcium : phosphorus ratio. The supplement can be fed in small quantities from three weeks of age onwards to accustom the foal to it before weaning.

Watch for signs of ill-health, colic, and poor appetite; seek veterinary advice if you are concerned. Attend to the umbilical cord of the orphan foal the same way as you do for a normal foal—that is, swab with tincture of iodine.

An orphan foal can become rather difficult to manage because he does not get his mother's discipline and has no herd position. Care and strictness in handling the foal is therefore important. Do not allow him to play games with you.

### Foster-mothering

Foster-mothering is the most convenient, easiest, and best method of rearing an orphan foal. It saves continuous feeding schedules, provides the foal with natural mare's milk, and satisfies its need for a mare's protection.

Select a mare that has lost her own foal within the previous twenty-four to forty-eight hours to ensure that she has not started drying off. If possible, single out a mare that has lost a young foal before she got used to it.

The age of the orphan should be about the same age as the foal lost. A quiet old mare with a good milk supply that has a foal at a similar age may be able and manageable enough to feed two foals. Young mares will not usually tolerate a second foal. An advertisement in a daily paper may help find a suitable foster-mare if one is not available locally.

Although methods vary considerably, here is a suggested basic method. Strip some milk from the mare as described previously for colostrum collection.

Allow the mare's udder to fill and become uncomfortable. Preferably the foal should be hungry. Rub some collected milk over the foal's head, nostrils, coat, and butt of tail and also rub some milk around the mare's own nostrils and muzzle.

Carefully control the mare and the foal when they are first introduced—two handlers are usually necessary. While holding the mare firmly and talking quietly to her, gently push the foal towards the mare's udder from the side, allowing the mare to sniff or lick the foal if she wishes. If the mare resents the foal back her into a corner and lift up one front leg while the foal is allowed to approach.

If the mare will not accept the foal with basic smell and sight recognition, extra measures can be taken. Sprinkle a small amount of salt over the foal's coat after the milk has been applied and allow the mare to lick the foal. Obtain some of the mare's fresh dung and rub some around the foal's legs and the butt of his tail.

Feed the foal for twenty-four hours on the mare's own milk stripped out by hand. This will give the orphan the digestive smell of the mare's own foal.

Use a twitch to restrain the mare only if all else fails. If the twitch fails, a tranquilliser injection given by a veterinary surgeon may calm the mare sufficiently to allow the foal to suck.

If the proposed foster-mother has just foaled, her afterbirth rubbed over the orphan may aid in acceptance. Skinning the mare's own dead foal and tying it over the orphan is a last resort and not usually warranted.

Once the mare has allowed the foal to have a drink, let the foal drink as much as he wants.

Remove the foal to an adjoining yard between feeds so that the mare can have communication with him. Reunite them if the mare shows signs of wanting him by whinnying, neighing, etc.

If the mare accepts the foal allow her to keep the foal with her, but observe them for the first two or three attempts at feeding. Watch for scours and other illness and seek veterinary advice if necessary.

On some studs, foals of little value from good milk-producing mares are destroyed or hand-reared so that the mare can act as a foster-mother to a valuable orphan foal should the necessity arise.